What leaders are saying about
The Forgotten Field . . .

I love it when authors are proven practitioners in the subjects they write about. Gerad has demonstrated that you can use multisite models to reach and transform rural communities. I am excited to see a spiritual awakening in rural America . . . maybe, just maybe, out of *The Forgotten Field* can come springs of revival to impact our nation!

Doug Clay
General Superintendent of the Assemblies of God
Springfield, Missouri

Everybody loves treasure! Through tenacious and insightful experience, Gerad Strong shows you where treasure resides in the rural community. His innovative approach reveals the reality, possibility, and strategy to engage an overlooked and impactful opportunity of ministry in the rural context.

Dr. Alan Bixler
Lead Pastor of Crosswalk Community Church
Founder and President of The Global Consultant
Sioux Falls, South Dakota

I had the privilege of watching the incubation and development of all the dreams written about in this book, and it has been a joy see them become a reality in Gerad and Melanie. This resource is a rich collection of information about multisite in a rural context that is enhanced by the author's own struggles and successes. You will be moved to possess a deeper burden for rural ministry and will become better equipped to walk it out as you read these pages.

Dr. Bryan Jarrett
Lead Pastor of Northplace Church
Director of The Water Tower Network
Sachse, Texas

There's substance and depth behind someone's words when they've lived what their writing about. As Gerad walks us through their story of multiplication in a rural context, he gives us a front row seat to the faith-igniting truths and practical applications that are necessary to transform communities. Whether you're part of the 60% of our nation who live in a rural setting or not, the principles in this book will help you and your church move boldly toward the fulfillment of Jesus' mandate to make disciples. I hear Gerad's voice as I read his words, and I'm inspired to lean further into learning, to choose courage, and to invite others to go with me on the adventure. I highly recommend this book to you!

Dr. Jeffery Portmann
Director, Church Multiplication Network—AG US
Springfield, Missouri

The rural context is ready for a new wave of Kingdom expansion. Gerad Strong's story and insights will ignite God-given dreams and provide a clear strategy for your ministry and leadership. From renewal to succession to rural multisite and leadership development, Gerad's book touches on each of your goals and dreams.

Scott Wilson
Global Pastor, Oaks Church
Author of *Impact: Releasing the Power of Influence*
Red Oak, Texas

There are many books that I have read over the years that have inspired me, challenged me, and informed me about ways to live and lead. Then there are others that you pick up that are both strategic and timely for the moment we are in today. Gerad Strong's book, *The Forgotten Field*, may just be one of those books for you. Gerad does an amazing job of weaving together his experience as the pastor of a multicampus church in South Dakota with the established patterns for effective multisite ministry. As the hearts of our nation are once again turned toward the needs and opportunities of rural America, this book can become a roadmap to one powerful way to plant life-giving churches.

Jeff Leake
Lead Pastor at Allison Park Church
Author of *Twelve Trends In Multiplication*
Pittsburgh, Pennsylvania

Gerad Strong is the real deal! His wisdom, insight, and love for ministry is that of a true rural, multisite pastor! He has been in the battle—and remains in the battle—to bring a spiritual revival to rural America through church planting.

Cody Cochran,
Lead Pastor of Bethel Assembly
Anson, Texas

For years, rural America has been an often-overlooked mission field. In this book, Gerad Strong demonstrates his passion for a harvest among the precious people who inhabit the smaller towns across the U.S. Speaking from experience, he describes multisite church models as viable approaches to bring quality ministry to rural areas. After giving 25 years of my life to a small town, I applaud Gerad's bold call to reach the millions in rural communities with the gospel.

Pastor Don Miller
Assemblies of God, So. Missouri District Superintendent
Springfield, Missouri

Most churches in the world are rural churches. In this book, Gerad Strong makes the case and lays out a strategy for effective church planting and revitalization in the rural context. Pastor Gerad is an incredible, visionary leader. If rural ministry is your passion, this book should be your next read!

Pastor Stephen Schaible
Assemblies of God, South Dakota District Superintendent
Sioux Falls, South Dakota

Potential is having or showing the capacity to develop into something in the future, and spiritual potential is when someone's giftings, wisdom, counsel, and obedience intersect with the power of the Holy Spirit, the leadership and Christ, and the favor of Father God. Throughout the pages of this book, you will see how marvelous God is when you release the courage to use your giftings, the strength to find wisdom and counsel, and the endurance to be standfast in obedience to His promise. On each page Gerad shares these valuable lessons, acquired through the Acts 2 Journey and Church Multiplication Network, to expand your horizon so you can experience the great conquest of your life. Allow your passion to be stirred, your vision to be clarified, and your values solidified for your journey. Each of you have the potential to conquer your fears and the spiritual potential to add to the Kingdom of God by fulfilling what God called you to do. Now, it's time to connect to your spiritual potential. Thanks, Gerad, for sharing your journey with us.

Rick Allen
National Men's & LFTL Director
Springfield, Missouri

In his book, Gerad Strong shares his understanding and approach to planting multisite rural churches. Through his personal insights and experiences, his book shares practical steps to launch and sustain successful multisite rural churches. Strong's journey began with a desire to see healthy churches established in rural communities, and he worked to see this desire become a reality. He sensed God's leading in launching rural multisite churches and shares principles from authors writing on the subject.

The Forgotten Field allows the reader to reflect on the multisite options and explore the idea with an open heart that sees multisite as *a* way, not *the* way, to strengthen churches in the rural communities.

Dwight Sandoz
Executive Director of Rural Advancement
Co-Director of Master of Arts Rural Ministry,
Trinity Bible College and Graduate School
Ellendale, North Dakota

I truly believe that God sent me an incredible gift the day I met Gerad Strong. We sensed God was calling us to plant a church in a rural community near us through multisite. Through strategic coaching, Gerad put us in a position to succeed. He helped me as the Lead Pastor in everything from buildings to community engagement to mentoring our campus pastor. I often recall the words of encouragement and prophetic prayer Gerad spoke over my life which led us to multiply as a church.

Sheldon McGorman
Lead Pastor of WCAG
Watford City, North Dakota

The
Forgotten
Field

The
Forgotten
Field

Using Multisite Models to Reach and Revive
Rural Communities with the Gospel

GERAD STRONG

Cover design and interior formatting
by Anne McLaughlin, Blue Lake Design, www.bluelakedesign.com

ISBN:
print: 978-1-947505-39-1 | *digital:* 978-1-947505-43-8

First printing 2022
Published by Baxter Press, Friendswood, Texas
Printed in the United States of America

TABLE OF CONTENTS

CHAPTER 1

TROUBLE

We were in a death spiral. Our church was 63 years old, and the median age of our members and attendees was even older. The senior pastor had decided to retire and asked me to become the Lead Pastor. At the time, I had only been the youth and associate pastor for four years, and now I was asked to pastor a plateaued and declining church. The situation looked bleak—we had so many needs, but few resources. My wife Melanie and I felt overwhelmed. We knew something had to shift for the survival of our well-established church, but we didn't know where to start.

When Melanie and I were voted in as Lead Pastors, we were filled with excitement, humility, and a strong sense of calling. However, those optimistic emotions quickly gave way to the sobering reality of our circumstances when an elderly couple approached one day and spoke a not-so-veiled threat: "Pastors come and go, but we'll always be here!" In other words, "Don't bother changing anything!"

How do you lead a church without creating change? It simply can't happen. I knew we needed renewal. We needed to replace or repair habits and traditions that were worn out, run-down, or broken. This journey began with a Spirit-empowered process that would expose our desperate need for change, and change accomplished two things: it propelled us to address our troubles in the church, and it surfaced many opportunities in our rural context.

Small-town America is in trouble because its churches are struggling. The myriad of reasons includes a new generation that finds the church to be irrelevant, an aging clergy with no succession plan, and a loss of vision within the local church. The common denominator is that these churches aren't prepared to grow and thrive. In the United States, 60 percent of American counties are classified as rural, and one in five Americans live in rural areas.[1] Additionally, rural communities are increasingly the focus of attention as people migrate out of cities in search of a simpler, slower, more meaningful life in the countryside.

Kristin Tate wrote an article in July of 2020 for the Rural Matters Institute where she observed that "a perfect storm of factors makes the decision to leave major cities like New York very obvious." She cited the spread of COVID in dense population centers, local government regulations, and remote working as three powerful factors that lure people away from metropolitan areas and into the suburbs and rural communities. Tate continued, "If the allure of cities declines further due to the risk of disease, a sputtering economy, and a future of telework, the flight to suburban and rural safety will continue well after a coronavirus vaccine hits the market."[2] Her predictions have proven true. Only a few decades ago, people flocked from farms to cities, but now, the flow is reversing. If rural remigration persists, the spiritual and social needs of rural communities will increase significantly beyond what they were before the pandemic.

Sociological challenges aren't the only threat to the life of rural churches. Psychological factors are also at play. Those who have taken up the pastoral mantle in a rural context (or wish to do so) face a deep-seated negative assumption that pastoring suburban or urban churches is more honorable than leading a rural congregation. In other words, we're often considered second-class spiritual leaders. As my friend and pastor, Dr. Bryan Jarrett, says, "Those who answer the call to move to the bush of Africa to spread the gospel are viewed as our heroes; however, those who settle on the plains or remote places of America are viewed as losers." This toxic perspective contributes to the perceived irrelevance of rural pastors, but it fails to acknowledge a wide-open mission field. Outside the population centers, next-generation leaders, church planters, factory workers, farmers, and ranchers are waiting for pastors who see their potential.

Some of the greatest spiritual heroes I've met have been the faithful pastors who serve in the rural areas of America. From their community integration to their faithfulness to open the church doors every week, these heroes are forged in the fires of serving when few notice them. However, many of these pastors are now retiring, often with no succession plan for their churches or personal assets to carry them into their sunset years. Some of them have held on too long because of those reasons, and their churches are unprepared for the next season. Nevertheless, the reality is painful. It's a sad state for those shepherds who faithfully stood in the breach for many years, and it's painful for the diminished congregations left in their communities.

Without a clear, compelling vision of a better future, some congregations are barely holding on. All they have are memories of yesterday, and focusing on the past has inadvertently overlooked the potential of the next generation. Many older church members long to see their grandchildren walk through the doors of a church, but the relevance of the church has faded. In the *Journal for the Scientific Study of Religion,* Mary Neitz observes that in many rural churches, only a few people keep the doors open. She calls these churches "the 'Faithful Remnant' congregations, where members remained faithful to their denominations and each other, despite declining numbers."[3] This "Faithful Remnant" displays rigorous persistence, which can be interpreted as stubbornness, but it can also be seen as faith-filled tenacity. Despite the faithfulness of this remnant, The Barna Group notes that "the majority of unchurched individuals (76 percent) have firsthand experience with one or more Christian churches and, based on that sampling, have decided they can better use their time in other ways."[4] This research highlights two opposite points. First, the faithful commitment of those in a rural church is to be commended and reproduced if possible. Second, the experience of the individuals who felt they could use their time better somewhere else speaks to the irrelevance of the church and the need for change.

The rural American landscape is littered with little white steeples that are now facing the reality of retiring pastors, almost empty buildings, and little to no prospects of the next generation entering the doors. However, if we look and listen carefully, we can detect a strong heartbeat in the rural communities of America. Not every rural town is drying up. There's still hope for vibrant spiritual life in every corner of American life: buildings waiting to be brought back to life, and shepherds waiting to be raised up and deployed to rural mission fields. Young people need to know the relevance of the gospel of Jesus Christ!

OPPORTUNITY

As I sat around a conference table in Dallas among a crowd of pastors who lead rural congregations across remote and forgotten places of America, God began to birth a vision in my heart. Some of those rural pastors had incredible dreams, but others were just trying to hold on one more year. As we interacted, I wrote down an idea God gave me that became a dream, and then a vision. (Alan Bixler, the first pastor I worked for, often told me, "If you can't write it down, you'll struggle to do it." I took his wisdom to heart, and I've written down crazy ideas and thoughts ever since!)

I was born and raised in western South Dakota, and my first lead pastorate was a church in my hometown. At every conference, on every podcast, and in every newsletter, I saw and heard what God was doing in big cities and suburban churches, and I wondered if God could do the same in my little part of the world. As I sat at the conference table in Dallas and questioned my contribution to God's kingdom, God redirected me to something I had written in my prayer journal almost six years earlier, before I became a Lead Pastor:

> I'm asking God for the grace, wisdom, and leadership to build a unified congregation that meets in multiple venues . . . bringing quality ministry and discipleship to those that are willing to journey from "come and see" to

"come and die" . . . providing ministry for communities
. . . building up leadership . . . developing leadership teams
that will reproduce and multiply in communities that are
underdeveloped . . . bringing it all under a unified banner
of vision, leadership, biblical teaching, and equipping.

Just over a year after sitting at the conference table in Dallas,
God opened the door of opportunity!

Our first additional campus was nestled in a little town of 700
people, located 81 miles from our primary location. The church
had a history longer than that of our own church, but over the
years it had lost much of its relevance, and its well-intended succession plans had stalled. It was being held together by six people,
and the prospect of hiring a future pastor was rapidly fading. Our
denominational district asked us if we would be interested in
adopting this congregation because it was the little church's only
hope of survival. If we didn't take it under our wing, the denomination was going to close the church.

I was reminded of Jesus' Parable of the Talents:

"For it will be like a man going on a journey, who called
his servants and entrusted to them his property. To one
he gave five talents, to another two, to another one, to
each according to his ability. Then he went away. He who
had received the five talents went at once and traded with
them, and he made five talents more. So also he who had
the two talents made two talents more. But he who had
received the one talent went and dug in the ground and
hid his master's money. Now after a long time the master
of those servants came and settled accounts with them.

And he who had received the five talents came forward, bringing five talents more, saying, 'Master, you delivered to me five talents; here, I have made five talents more.' His master said to him, 'Well done, good and faithful servant. You have been faithful over a little; I will set you over much. Enter into the joy of your master.' And he also who had the two talents came forward, saying, 'Master, you delivered to me two talents; here, I have made two talents more.' His master said to him, 'Well done, good and faithful servant. You have been faithful over a little; I will set you over much. Enter into the joy of your master.' He also who had received the one talent came forward, saying, 'Master, I knew you to be a hard man, reaping where you did not sow, and gathering where you scattered no seed, so I was afraid, and I went and hid your talent in the ground. Here, you have what is yours.' But his master answered him, 'You wicked and slothful servant! You knew that I reap where I have not sown and gather where I scattered no seed? Then you ought to have invested my money with the bankers, and at my coming I should have received what was my own with interest. So take the talent from him and give it to him who has the ten talents.'" (Matthew 25:14-28, ESV)

In our case, I believe God was looking to see what we would do with the talents He placed in our hands. If we would do something with this struggling little church 81 miles away, maybe, just maybe, God would entrust us with more.

Only two years later, weekly attendance at the little church had blossomed into more than ten percent of the community's population. (In rural ministry, we use percentages because they are more meaningful than raw numbers.) That was the first step in God fulfilling the vision He had given us, and we jumped in with all our might!

The Parable of the Talents applies to all of us. The Master, Jesus, has placed something in your hands. What will you do with it? My hope is that you will multiply what God has placed in you and ask the Lord for something bigger than you can do on your own. In this book, I hope to encourage you and give you some handles to begin your journey toward your God-given assignment!

CHAPTER 2

BACK TO BASICS

I once heard that a healthy church should see salvations and water baptisms on a regular basis. We know this is foundational to the purpose of the Church, but it can also feel like an impossible mission. Each year as we filled out our denomination's Annual Church Ministries Report (ACMR), we realized we were not fulfilling the Great Commission. We rarely saw these markers of spiritual health, so we began to change how we pursued them.

The question we began to ask was: Are we healthy? We continued to ask it when we took on our first campus.

We had to get back to basics if we were going to turn our plateaued and declining church around. We began to celebrate people, ministries, and our vision, and the cultural change was immediately noticeable. The following year we experienced an 87 percent increase in recorded salvations and a 400 percent increase in water baptisms! Celebrating healthy markers like salvation and water baptisms reinforced another principle: We need to "measure what matters." Attendance matters because each number is a soul. Guest retention matters because it indicates whether visitors feel welcomed into the family. As we began to measure what matters, we were able to have heartfelt celebrations, and we found areas of our ministry that needed improvement. For example, we noticed we were giving too little attention to the Holy Spirit. We had to change that! We began to provide special ministry services focused on the nature and role of the Holy Spirit.

Evaluating the church can be a painful and sobering process, but measuring will inevitably reveal well-intentioned ministries that are no longer bearing fruit. We had a choice: update them, eliminate them, or replace them. As time passed, fruit began to return, and we put a special emphasis on leadership development, that is, making disciples. As we called congregants to lead and issued the call to serve, people answered, and spiritual growth became both normal and thrilling. Additionally, as health began to return to our church, adding more congregations became possible because we had something healthy to reproduce.

In recent years, the concept of multisite has grown from fledgling attempts into a genuine movement. Many articles and books have been written to describe the phenomenon.[5] However, little material is available for providing a multisite model in the rural context. I wouldn't presume that a multisite church model is *the* answer to rural church problems, but I believe it is at least *a* solution to help rural churches grow in size and impact.

I will use the definition of multisite given by Geoff Surratt, Greg Ligon, and Warren Bird: Multisite is a "church that shares a common vision, budget, leadership, and board."[6] I would also add that a multisite church is one church that meets in various locations and venues. In urban settings, *multisite* has traditionally been synonymous with *megachurch*,[7] but it is becoming a model that is used in various settings and church sizes.[8] However, one area which has been overlooked is the rural setting, where populations may not be dense, but the residents are still people who need Jesus.[9] Donnie Griggs discusses the oversight of rural America in the opening of his book, *Small Town Jesus*. He summarizes an urban or city view of the people who call rural America home, and he quotes Princeton professor Robert Wuthnow:

> Relatively little research has been devoted to small towns since the 1950's. . . . small towns were viewed as part of a declining sector populated by fewer people, and of interest more as the location of food production and tourism than as places where people lived. As a result, data has been available from census reports about the number, size, demographic composition, and economic characteristics of small towns, but little effort has been made to learn what residents of small towns think or believe.[10]

Wuthnow illustrates the oversight of rural America, but there are encouraging findings within some multisite research. Research by The Barna Group has revealed a spectrum of church types that choose to become multisite. There may be an assumption that most of the churches that use a multisite model are relatively young organizations; however, Barna Group found that one in four multisite churches were over 100 years old when they launched their first multisite campus or church plant.

Additionally, the number of adult attendees across multisite churches range from eighteen to twenty-five thousand per weekend.[11] Surratt, Ligon, and Bird reinforce Barna Group research by stating, "The multi-site phenomenon is growing dramatically among churches of all sizes, bringing it soon enough to every city, every denomination, and every style of ministry."[12]

Increasingly, multisite is becoming an accepted model in rural locations. Proof may be found in stories like my personal experience, which I will share in later chapters, and in a recent publication by Leadership Network:

> Another big surprise of the survey was how many churches (47%) have a campus in a small town or rural area. A Montana church opened its first multisite location in a rural location instead of in a larger city. A Texas congregation is reaching into multiple small towns, because there aren't any larger cities within a three-hour drive. A North Carolina multisite leader notes: "We are reaching people in smaller markets and rural areas outside large cities."[13]

However, I find little indication the multisite church model is being well utilized in rural America. Although Surratt, Ligon, and Bird enhance Barna Group's research, I disagree with their inclusive comment about "every style of ministry" for two reasons. First, according to the survey, there are 251 multisite churches that have a campus in a rural context.[14] Dave Travis, former head of Leadership Network, cites a Duke University survey estimating that 8,000 churches are currently practitioners of multisite.[15] When we compare the two numbers, we find that only three percent of the current multisite churches have a rural footprint. Second, even for the multisite churches in the rural context, the gap of information, encouragement, and validity is significantly lacking. Therefore, we can conclude that rural ministry has not yet become a significant focus for a multisite church model.

In the way I've made my case so far, I may sound like an overlooked rural guy with a chip on his shoulder, but I really just want to say that rural is a viable place for a multisite church model. As I've ventured into this territory of multisite, I'm encouraged by the friendships I've made along the way. Let me tell you about a few of them.

Cody Cochran is pastor of Bethel, a rural multisite in West Texas. Cody and Bethel Assembly have answered the call to multiply. He remarked, "We decided to do multisite because we saw many of the churches across all denominations that were either closing in rural towns or had lost all of their life and hope. We felt like what the Lord was doing at Bethel was special and needed to be replicated." Today, they have four campuses in communities ranging in population from 2000 to 8000. Some of their campuses are reaching 25 percent of the community!

Another friend and pastor, Chris Brewer, serves in rural Arkansas. He and his church chose to multiply because they "wanted to reach more people." Currently, they serve two communities. They launched their second campus in the middle of the pandemic, and although it was difficult, they've seen God bless their ministry. Chris and his church have seen their attendance and giving triple!

Sheldon McGorman is a pastor just beginning the journey as a rural multisite in North Dakota. Sheldon and his church are currently in the process of planting their second campus in rural Montana. Their church family has a bold vision to provide resources and take the gospel to a community over 70 miles away. Sheldon recently told me that he realized his journey was possible because I had already taken the leap into a rural multisite.

There's something powerful about knowing it can be done, and I hope my story and these courageous pastors inspire you to believe you can do it too!

CHAPTER 3

THE NEED AND THE VISION

In a small rural town, far, far away, Andy slowly assists Aunt Bee into their church on a beautiful Sunday morning. The piano begins to play, and everyone opens their hymnals instinctively to number 86, "How Great Thou Art." Although the singing is a bit off-key, hearts are full as worship fills the church and the small congregation moves through their favorite songs. With the conclusion of the hymns, everyone takes their seats, and Aunt Bee scans the room looking for Opie, hoping this would be the Sunday he would come to church again. When she doesn't see him, she turns her attention to the platform where her elderly pastor steadies himself.

The pastor solemnly stands behind the pulpit with his hands gripping the sides of the worn wood. He clears his throat and says, "I would like to make an announcement before I open the Word today." He stutters as he begins to lift his voice. "I've loved these 35 years of service to you and the beautiful people of Mayberry. You and the people of this community have been my life's work, and I'm thankful for every moment of it. I'm not sure how to say this, so I might as well just get to the point: Today, I'm announcing my retirement."

When he says the word "retirement," the room gasps, and the minister calmly motions for his small congregation to settle down. Andy and Aunt Bee look around the room at the few faithful congregants, wondering what is to come next. Tears begin to roll down Aunt Bee's cheek as the pastor soberly opens his Bible to the passage he would preach that morning.

Everybody realizes that their little church—and the town of Mayberry—are in trouble.

This scene is, of course, reminiscent of *The Andy Griffith Show*, but this scenario is playing out in rural churches throughout the country. Rural communities are suffering spiritually. In his book, *The Forgotten Church: Why Rural Ministry Matters for Every Church In America*, Glenn Daman writes, "Rural America is rapidly becoming a spiritual wasteland, where churches are being closed because they are overlooked and cast aside by the larger church community."[16] Daman's statement seems broad and accusatory, yet I believe his opinion is supported by recent research.

In 2016, the Rural Matters Institute, a community for pastors and Christian leaders serving in non-urban contexts, conducted research to examine the spiritual condition of rural North America. The research offered a county-by-county report of religious trends. Much of the data collected was from the 2010 U.S. Religion Census.[17] These findings were presented by Tena

Stone and Chrissy Schaeffer at the Rural Matters Conference in September of 2017.[18] Within the research, adherents to religious groups were labeled "claimed" individuals, while those who have no participation in any religious group were labeled "unclaimed." Stone and Schaeffer note that high numbers of "unclaimed" individuals live in rural counties in the United States. To demonstrate this fact, 12 non-metro U.S. counties were randomly selected. In these random non-metro counties, the percentage of the population that is "unclaimed" ranges from 8.7 percent to 79.0 percent, resulting in an average percentage of "unclaimed" at approximately 50 percent.[19]

Stone and Schaeffer's research supports Daman's statement of the spiritual condition of the rural context. Approximately 50 percent of rural individuals don't have any religious affiliation, which highlights the need for further evangelism there. A possible solution to reach these "unclaimed" individuals is a multisite church model.

Scott McConnel, author of *Multi-Site Churches: Guidance for the Movement's Next Generation*, stated, "Multi-site churches are evangelistic. They have experienced growth and are growth oriented." McConnel quotes Chuck Carter, whom he labels as a "first-generation multi-site pastor" (one of the first pastors to move a church toward multi-site in North America): "There has got to be something driving the thing [multisite]. Among the churches I know where it is successful, it is because the Great Commission is driving it."[20] Multisite churches focus on evangelism and have a desire to pursue "unclaimed" people in every context.

When I read this insight, I began to wonder how many "unclaimed" people are in my area. It was a sobering consideration, based on sheer statistics and probability. Our area had more cattle than people, and we're not alone. Many people, who are widely scattered across the rural counties, have no connection to Jesus—or any religion, for that matter. After researching all the counties where we believed a healthy church could be planted, I discovered that over 140,000 people in my region were "unclaimed," meaning they had no religious affiliation. My perception of small-town America was shattered by the realization that there were so many within driving distance of my own home whose eternity is bleak. Mayberry is, indeed, in big trouble!

(A valuable resource to help you investigate the religious condition of a county is www.thearda.com. This resource collects data from the census and compiles it from a religious standpoint.)

The need of our region was the perfect soil for planting a vision, so I began to share my observations and my burden with our leadership. I was sure that in time, God would do something wonderful and powerful. One day while I was in prayer, I kept sensing the phrase, "seventy times seven." At first I thought I might have forgiveness issues I needed to deal with (because in Matthew 18 Jesus tells Peter to forgive "more than seventy times seven"). But as I continued in prayer, it hit me: Our church was just hitting 68 years old. I thought, *Surely, God, You're not asking us to have seven church locations by the time we turn 70 years old!* I can have some crazy ideas, and this one certainly seemed to qualify as over the top and outside the box. I held this prayer close, not telling anyone but Melanie. She's the realist in the family, and when she felt that it could be from the Lord, I knew God was up to something big!

A few weeks later I was walking through the lobby of the church, and one of my elders, Dave, stopped me. He said, "Pastor, I'm excited for our future campuses. I'm praying for our future!"

I replied, "Me too!"

As I started to walk away, Dave added, "Pastor, God told you seven campuses, didn't He?"

Dave didn't know anything about my prayer time or my conversation with Melanie. His supernatural insights and his words of affirmation confirmed that my "crazy" sense of God's leading wasn't a result of bad pizza I'd eaten the night before. This brief conversation was the catalyst that propelled me to get serious about a timeline to launch our church in a visionary adventure.

The vision was exciting, but it would require us to become even more strategic and intentional with our limited resources of finances and people. I looked for a mentor to help me lead our church where I'd never been before. At the time, Chris Railey was the Director of the Church Multiplication Network, and he coached me to create a detailed plan. This wasn't just a sterile document; Chris helped me see the sequence of steps that were needed to make ideas into a plan and the plan into reality. (For more information about CMN, go to Churchmultiplication.net.) The document gradually took shape and was revised several times as our faith grew and we found new resources along the way. When we had the vision plan drafted and the elders were united around the vision and plan, we went public.

I'll never forget the Sunday we shared our vision. I'm not sure I remember a time when I was more nervous. I knew that the minute I stated the vision publicly, there would be no turning back. When I shared our vision with the congregation, the people went nuts! People really are hungry for vision and want to be a part of something bigger than themselves. The following week, our staff team went to our denomination's District Council (district/state clergy meetings). Other church leaders were at the event, and the word had already spread about our multisite vision. Not unexpectedly, we got mixed reviews. (Listen, not everyone will be on board with what you're doing. Push past the naysayers and late adaptors, and follow where God leads you.)

Most of the people in our church instantly realized that the need was so great that we couldn't afford to falter. Countless people are "unclaimed" and need to experience the saving power of Jesus. The younger generation needs to discover a Creator who sent His Son for them—and you are the visionary answer to that need! Seek the Lord, and He will impart to you something far bigger than you could dream up yourself! Like Mordecai inspired Esther, I challenge you to not keep quiet, because who knows, perhaps you were made "for such a time as this" (Esther 4:14).

CHAPTER 4

WORKABLE MODELS

Changing from a single site to multisite cannot be a haphazard move. It's a deliberate action preceded by plenty of research, planning, vision casting, fundraising, and leadership development. To help you discover a multisite model that's right for you—if, in fact, that's how God is leading you—I want to give you an overview of multisite church models. We will also look at motivations, biblical views, and potential problems of a multisite church model. From subcategories of structure, age, and size, we will look at a broad overview.

SUBCATEGORIES

Brad House and Gregg Allison have identified seven models of churches, five of which they consider multisite. Let's take a closer look at those five.

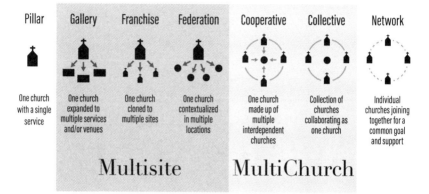

- The **Gallery** model is simply a church with multiple services. The services can be identical or offer a variety of worship styles, language options, etc.

- The **Franchise** model is one church cloned to multiple sites. Think about a corporation like McDonald's, where each location looks, feels, and sounds the same, and offers the same products. Within this model, decision-making and branding flow from a centralized authority, preventing the local leadership from diverging from the model.

- The **Federation** model is one church contextualized in multiple locations. This model offers room for the local leadership to adapt to specific needs in their communities. It has two leadership teams: the one at the central campus and the local staff teams that serve the various campuses.

- The **Cooperative** model is a co-op organization of churches that voluntarily connect for mutual benefit, for example, in the area of financial management.

- And the **Collective** model is a group of churches collaborating as one church. The participating churches gather to work on common projects, but without a common internal structure.

Each of these five models functions differently, yet all of them fall into the multisite church model, according to House and Allison. The subcategories are differentiated by the placement of power and control. House and Allison define this as the "locus of power," which is the "authority and the responsibility to establish vision, make decisions, and spend money." Power and control are *centralized* in the Gallery, Franchise, and Federation models, while power and control are *distributed* to each site in the Cooperative and Collective models. When power and control of the vision, decisions, and money are placed centrally, they may be perceived positively or negatively, depending on the strategy.[21]

In my rural ministry context, we operate as a Federation Model. We centralize budgets but leave the details about spending the budget to the discretion of the campus pastor.[22] Additionally, vision is centralized, but flexibility allows each church freedom to strategize for how best to accomplish the vision in its specific locality. The decision for where power is placed rests on the overall strategy of a multisite church, which is illustrated in the following section.

STRATEGIES

Beyond these five subcategories of operation, we also find different strategies, which are defined by the Barna Group. Their study identifies five separate strategies within the activity and operations of multisite models:

- Multisite Beginners: a single church with two or three total locations or campuses.

- Planting Beginners: two or three semi-independent churches, where the "daughter" churches are considered church plants.

- Multisite Strategists: a single church with four or more total locations or campuses.

- Planting Strategists: four or more semi-independent churches, where the "daughter" churches are considered church plants.

- Location Partners: a separate congregation meeting at, and sharing resources with, another church (for example, a ministry reaching a specific demographic group, such as a young adult congregation or an international group with services in a different language). [23]

In a study of 222 churches, Barna Group found 24 percent were multisite strategists, 20 percent were planting strategists, 17 percent were multisite beginners, 21 percent were planting beginners, and 18 percent were location partners. The research and distribution within this study looks like this:

Total Number of Church Locations
Strategists

4 sites
—Multisite Strategists: 30
—Planting Strategists: 30

5 sites

—Multisite Strategists: 13

—Planting Strategists: 20

6 to 10 sites

—Multisite Strategists: 23

—Planting Strategists: 34

11 or more sites

—Multisite Strategists: 36

—Planting Strategists: 16

Beginners and Location Partners

2 sites

—Multisite Beginners: 16

—Planting Beginners: 48

—Location Partners: 66

3 sites

—Multisite Beginners: 84

—Planting Beginners: 52

—Location Partners: 34

This research reveals two insights: First, a church labeled "strategist" suggests the intentionality of vison, planning, and execution. While "beginner" should not necessarily imply a less purposeful approach, it may mean that the leaders chose a strategy out of necessity rather than intentionality. These necessities could include unexpected growth, building issues, and leadership changes. However, power and control decisions appear to determine each church's operational strategy. From multisite strategists to planting strategists, power and control reflect the spectrum of dependence found between church sites. The strategy selected is not only based on the number of locations or power and control, but also on several other factors, including attendance, timing, financial stability, and expectations. Churches with higher weekend attendance fell within the multisite strategists and planting strategists.

Although Barna Group does not offer a reason for this data, I would suggest it's again reflective of the intentionality of vision, planning, and execution found in the "strategists'" behavior. As to timing, older churches were more likely to move toward multisite when they hit critical mass in their attendance or experienced a change in leadership. Additionally, finances became stable within three to five years across each of the multisite strategies. Finally, it appears that the leader's expectations of managing a multisite ministry are common among these churches. A multisite church leader was uncomfortable through the initial expansion; however, the leader became more comfortable as the network grew beyond five and six locations.[24]

While we were operating our first three campuses, it was a daunting task to think strategically about multiple locations. With every sermon series, every outreach, every major holiday, and every additional staff member, I felt unsure and uncomfortable, but when we moved past our fourth campus and eventually had seven, leading became a much easier task because our mindset had adjusted, effective systems were in place, and complexity had become normalized.

An analysis of the multiple subcategories and strategies reflects the way a church functions. As we've seen, these factors are shaped by power and control, attendance, timing, finances, and the intentions of the leader. Therefore, churches moving from a single site to multisite must consider these variables to effectively become a church in multiple locations. Take the time to determine where you will place the power and control. What's the right model for your leadership and your ministry context?

AGE AND SIZE

Many of us dismiss what the Lord may want to do through our ministries because we think our congregation is too old or too small. That's simply a lie that will rob you of your God-given assignment.

As we saw earlier, Geoff Surratt, Greg Ligon, and Warren Bird expand on Barna Group research by stating, "The multisite phenomenon is growing dramatically among churches of all sizes, bringing it soon enough to every city, every denomination, and every style of ministry."[25] With the increase of technology and rural remigration due to the pandemic, I believe multisite is becoming an accepted model in rural locations.

If you still have questions about the various strengths and weaknesses of each model, that's entirely normal. Talk to people who have done it, find resources like the Church Multiplication Network (CMN), and ask a mentor or coach to help you wade into this process to determine if it's right for you and your church.

CHAPTER 5

HOW MULTISITE CAN WORK

Discovering how a multisite model works begins with asking the right questions. Good leaders ask *great* questions, and great leaders ask the *right* questions. Over the years, I've worked really hard at asking the right questions. Several are below.

1. Am I truly called to this endeavor?

You need to wrestle with this personal question. If you aren't called, you'll quit when it gets hard—and trust me, it will get hard. Personally, I believe many people are called to lead and multiply their churches. The harvest remains plentiful, but the workers, still, are few. However, if you don't personally feel called to this endeavor, it's okay. Find people who are and champion them!

2. Am I planting a sovereign church or a campus church?

Before you create your plan, determine if you will birth churches to become sovereign (stand-alone) or remain part of your church network as a campus. There's nothing wrong with birthing sovereign churches, but you need to determine this now, before you begin implementing your strategy. A multiplying church can operate either way. In this book, I won't be discussing how to launch sovereign churches, although it's not very different from the launch of a multisite church campus. It's the mindset and culture created on the front end of the journey that separates the two.

3. Do I have a workable vision plan?

A vision plan is the strategy you and your leadership will execute. Jesus warned us to think before we act: "Suppose one of you wants to build a tower. Won't you first sit down and estimate the cost to see if you have enough money to complete it? For if you lay the foundation and are not able to finish it, everyone who sees it will ridicule you, saying, 'This person began to build and wasn't able to finish'" (Luke 14:28-30). The vision plan defines the scope, including a visionary statement (your why), location(s), leadership development plans, budgets, fundraising, timelines, etc. We will go into further detail on the vision plan in the Nuts and Bolts chapter.

4. Do I have a rider for the horse?

The church is about people—not buildings or budgets. Every horse (a church campus) needs a rider (a campus pastor). Whether your vision is to have one or seven campuses, do you have a rider (or at least a pipeline to develop a rider) for each one?

As you know, pastoring is hard, and many are leaving the ministry every day. I believe the American church has failed to passionately and regularly issue the call to ministry, but you and I can change that. Men and women in your congregation are waiting to not only be deployed as missionaries in their workplace, but also to be challenged to consider the call to vocational or bi-vocational ministry. Paul wrote Timothy, "Here is a trustworthy saying: Whoever aspires to be an overseer desires a noble task" (1 Timothy 3:1). Do they know they're needed?

5. Is my church worth reproducing?

Anything can be reproduced, but not everything needs to be. Not all churches are healthy and worthy to serve as a model. If you wouldn't attend your church if you weren't the pastor, your church isn't reproducible. Multisite will magnify the good and the bad in the DNA of your church's culture. If your people aren't welcoming, your campuses won't be welcoming. If your church isn't focused on the community, your campuses won't be focused on the community. Even on a smaller scale, if your church and leadership team aren't good at communicating with each other, adding more locations will only magnify the problem. Trust me, I learned the hard way. Your plans for multisite may need to be put on hold until you can solve significant problems in your culture and DNA. We'll address any need to change the culture in chapter ten.

6. Do I have someone I can share this burden with?

If you're reading this book, it means you probably have a burden. And in the earliest stages of formulating a multisite plan, you need to be cautious about who you include in your planning.

The vision is fragile and not everyone can see what you see. Still, you shouldn't attempt to bear the weight alone. Have at least one trustworthy person (i.e., your spouse, an elder, or a mentor) with whom you can share your ideas, joys, frustrations, and dreams.

7. Am I willing to stay long enough to see this vision through?

We don't need any more orphaned churches. Launching this endeavor won't be a quick or easy journey. Don't be surprised if it takes several years . . . or even decades. Be sure of God's calling, do your homework, plan effectively, build leaders, and communicate clearly and often. You'll need firm ground under you when you experience pushback . . . and it's coming!

Finding the answers to these questions proved crucial in fulfilling the vision God gave our church. I hope they will be helpful as you move forward with your own vision.

CHAPTER 6

PUSHBACK

If you decide to walk down the road of multisite, you need to expect opposition. The best strategy is to know what the opposition is saying, be aware of the common (but misguided) assumptions many have about multisite churches, and head off those complaints before they do serious damage. Below are some of the most common forms of resistance you can expect.

"Pastors Can't Know Their People."

Some people believe that a pastor should personally know each person who sits under his or her ministry. This concern stems partially from multisite operations that use video technology to replace clergy preaching at each location. I would argue that successful preaching isn't solely based on knowing a leader personally, but instead, it's based on sound biblical delivery. To support this argument, Warren Bird describes the ways the gospel is being received in other ways beyond in-person delivery:

"I believe that these Bible teachers [Bird's childhood pastor and guest pastors] all could have taught via video if the technology had existed, just as people have come to faith by watching a Billy Graham telecast or listening to a recording from one of yesteryear's great gospel communicators."[26] He suggests the effectiveness of a sound biblical delivery can be powerful in the lives of those who don't know the pastor. Additionally, in the multisite model, pastors shepherd each location with ongoing discipleship and pastoral care, which reaches beyond the weekend preaching and services.[27]

"Multisite Makes Church a Spectacle."

Some people believe that multisite makes the church into little more than a spectacle. They complain: "The focus in multisites is often on the event more than the community, and people come for the show without connecting to the community." I disagree. I don't believe there is credible evidence to suggest that the focus is more on the event than the people. Without community, a church of any size or style wouldn't exist very long. Bird affirms this view: "In our observations and conversations, we've learned that multi-site must build community or they die."[28] Surveys by Leadership Network show that multisite churches are having a profound evangelistic impact, and those impacts can only occur through a healthy community that reaches beyond the weekend experience.[29]

"There's No Biblical Basis for Multisite."

An article written by Jonathan Leeman raises yet another concern about multisite: "There is no clear example of a multisite church in the New Testament, only supposition."[30] Leeman's

thinking suggests that those in favor of multisite are merely grasp-
ing in the Scriptures for something that's not there. On the other
hand, Brad House and Gregg Allison argue that the first church
was a multisite church. They describe the primary day-to-day
functions within the Christian church in the book of Acts:

> The church in Jerusalem met day-to-day in a central
> location and the disciples' homes. In the large gathering
> place of the temple, the apostles preached and performed
> signs and wonders, and the believers enjoyed fellowship,
> gave sacrificially, worshiped, and prayed. Likewise, in the
> smaller gatherings in homes, the apostles taught and did
> miracles, and the disciples lived in the community, helped
> other disciples and the poor, worshiped, and prayed. This
> dual-structured gathering occurred regularly.[31]

The authors argue that the book of Acts points to the church
of Jerusalem meeting in the temple and in homes. Their inter-
pretation is that the larger Christian church of Jerusalem met in
various locations, yet it still functioned as one body, so the church
could be considered an early version of a multisite model. Perhaps
both perspectives are right. Leeman suggests that the people were
gathered together in one place. His understanding of Acts 2:46,
5:12, and 6:2 shapes his thinking. House and Allison also use
Acts 2:46 to make their point, with additional passages from the
books of Acts and Romans:

> "And day by day, attending the temple together and
> breaking bread in their homes, they received their food
> with glad and generous hearts." (Acts 2:46 ESV)

John Piper was the Lead Pastor of Bethlehem Baptist, a church originally organized in 1871. The church went multisite in 2002 after Piper concluded that "the Bible neither forbids nor mandates" multisite ministry.[32] Forbidding something would imply a banning of such an activity, which would suggest it was a sin. I would argue that a multisite church model is neither a sin nor a mandate. The early church functioned much like a multisite church; however, I agree with Piper in that there are no mandates for this model.

The description found in the book of Acts depicts the necessity of meeting in various places due to logistics, growth, and needs. If the early church used multiple locations to meet the needs of the people, then how can it be a sin to do the same today? House and Allison support this perspective by addressing the multiple locations found in the early church through both Jerusalem and Rome.[33] They reference Acts 12:12 (ESV), which states, "[Peter] went to the house of Mary, the mother of John whose other name was Mark, where many were gathered together and were praying." This text suggests ministry taking place in a home. Additionally, Darrell Gaines argues for various locations of the early church:

> The Jerusalem church met "in the temple and . . . from house to house" (Acts 2:46, NASB). Paul refers to "the church in the house" of someone four times (Rom. 16:5; 1 Cor. 16:19; Col. 4:15; Phile. 2). Paul taught "publicly and from house to house" (Acts 20:20). . . . Part of the purpose for this section is to demonstrate the kind of argument multi-site proponents could be referencing to bolster their position.[34]

We see a similar pattern in the book of Romans. Paul wrote at the conclusion of the letter, "Greet also the church in their house. Greet my beloved Epaenetus, who was the first convert to Christ in Asia" (Romans 16:5 ESV). Additionally, various other passages of Scripture may be cited to support a multisite perspective (for example, Acts 5:42; Acts 18:7-8; Romans 16:14-15; Colossians 4:15; 1 Corinthians 14:23; and 1 Corinthians 16:15).

Gaines reviews the work of various scholars which point toward early Christians meeting in homes.[35] He also highlighted that larger assemblies of people would have met in wealthier members' homes because those homes could accommodate a larger group of people. Gaines stated, "If church meetings normally took place in homes in the New Testament era, and if these homes could only hold a relatively small number of people (as is often argued), then we can expect that citywide churches consisted of multiple house groups. One could see why this might be viewed as precedent for multi-site."[36] Therefore, it is my opinion that the supporting narrative found in Acts and Romans affirms that multisite is a viable option and certainly not a sin.

I may not have heard all the objections to launching a multisite church in a rural area, but I've heard many of them. Honestly, I'm thrilled that people ask hard questions because they prompt me to think more deeply, talk with more experts, and pray harder that God would give us His clear direction as we plan and dream about the future of our church.

CHAPTER 7

POTENTIAL PROBLEMS

Beyond the theological debate of multisite, there are other potential problems. As previously stated, a model is a system used as an example to follow or imitate, but deficiencies may be discovered when attempting to replicate the original design. And if the original model of ministry has flaws, they will be not only replicated, but magnified. David D'Angelo and Ryan Stigile begin their book with the warning that multisite can create more problems than it solves. They make it clear: "Multisite will multiply exactly who you are today. Nothing more. Nothing less."[37] They assert that when a multisite grows, it's not only the positive qualities of the church that are passed along.

From my personal ministry experience, I agree.[38] With each location added, everything multiplies. For example, with each added location there are additional church budgets to be managed, children's ministries to be resourced, additional equipment needed for technology, and social media platforms to be operated. Every church has good and bad qualities, and every kind of growth accentuates those qualities. For example, if information isn't communicated clearly, accurately, and consistently, each additional church location will only worsen that communication. I discovered this deficit in my church when we added the second location.[39] The church staff and I were accustomed to communicating in the same office and building complex where it was simple enough to clarify any confusion. But when we added an additional office and building complex 81 miles away, the weaknesses in our communication skills were soon exposed.

LEADERSHIP DEVELOPMENT

Another potential problem is identifying and developing leaders. The leadership of any organization is vital, and even more so in the church, which relies so much on intrinsic motivation. Carol Alexander states, "The Church needs well-equipped leaders that realize the importance and extent of this mission, and understand the enterprise to which they are committed."[40] The mission of the church is to reach people with the revelation and love of Jesus Christ through quality leadership that's adequately equipped, but poor leadership can be magnified within a multisite church model. D'Angelo and Stigile highlight this problem:

> [Churches] spend more time planning and dreaming about the campus *launch* than they do preparing for the entire ministry *season* [daily ministry to follow the launch]. Before long, they find themselves short on staff,

stretched for time, and lacking the systems they need to lead people to next steps.[41]

I agree with their observation. My church failed to prepare properly for the launch of a campus in Kadoka, South Dakota, a small town about 120 miles away.[42] The campus pastor wasn't properly vetted and proved unequipped to handle the day-to-day stress of the ministry. I don't blame them; it was my fault for making too many assumptions and moving too quickly.

House and Allison state, "Multisite has the unfortunate advantage of helping churches to expand faster than the leadership can grow to lead them."[43] Carol Alexander adds that "the Church in the West is in decline, and ill-equipped Christian leaders who have not been strategic in spiritual, intellectual and creative leadership have left a vacuous gap that must now be filled."[44]

Within the context of multisite, I agree. It takes strategic leadership to pursue this vision, yet it also takes a thoughtful, shrewd leader who prepares for the multiplication of every aspect of a multisite ministry. Ill-equipped leaders are a real problem for any church, but a multisite model magnifies the shortcomings of an ill-equipped leader. This point is illustrated by my experience planting new campuses and is further supported by D'Angelo and Stigile:

> One of the most significant pitfalls lies within the Campus Pastor. Leadership sets the tone and pace for any organization. You can have the best strategy, the most precise plan, and the most excellent resources, but if you do not identify and invest in the right leaders for each campus, you are setting yourself up for frustration and failure.[45]

D'Angelo, Stigile, and Alexander agree that Christian leadership within the church, and especially a multisite church, must be adequately equipped to stay focused on the mission and handle the expanding needs. This preparation is non-negotiable. Don't press on without it.

DECISIONS AND STRUCTURE

A multisite church model is predicated on replication in multiple campuses, and it's crucial to place godly, competent leaders at each site. D'Angelo and Sigile address this concern: "When a church goes multisite without clearly defining a central leader for each ministry area, it is a setup to experience a number of challenges."[46]

Each leader that presides over a specific area of ministry for the whole organization (for example, children's ministry) must organize, clarify, and manage expectations of ministry at each campus. I would argue that a multisite church model usually functions best with a central services model, which may be defined as "making and enforcing decisions of brand, vision, finances, staff, and programs."[47] Without such centralized leadership, unwanted and unnecessary problems develop. Critical meetings are missed. Growth objectives are unmet. Feedback from campuses is not processed. Key talking points aren't replicated. Mission and vision dissipate over time.[48]

Without accountability from a dedicated, responsible leader, problems inevitably develop within the structure of replication. A multisite strategy may get away with decentralized leadership for a while, but when it prepares to launch beyond three campuses, it needs to commit to a centralized leadership structure. D'Angelo and Stigile state:

> It is important to be establishing a centralized leadership team. These ministry leaders no longer work for a specific campus but instead take responsibility for resourcing all campuses with strategies and ministry plans. They also continue coaching campus leaders in their areas. This sets you up with a structure that can truly scale as the organization continues to grow.[49]

As a church intentionally becomes a multisite strategist (a single church with four or more campuses), it may be able to properly address challenges only through a centralized services model. Instead of a luxury, it becomes a necessity.

DECISION MAKING

Beyond the servicing of multisite campuses, the decision-making framework can be challenging. As a multisite church model grows more complex, so does decision-making. Without proper delegation of decision-making, varying levels of leadership may not develop properly. D'Angelo and Sigile observe, "Decision-making is a part of developing as a leader. When only a select few make decisions of consequence, only a select few are fully developing."[50]

In looking at the greater care and development of a multisite church model, House and Allison align with D'Angelo and Sigile: "Good leadership relinquishes control in order to foster collective ownership, thereby spreading out the care for the organization among several people."[51] Spreading out the decision-making process produces a higher level of leadership development and quality of care for each congregation. Without a sound, clear decision-making framework, the structure can become a headache for those who are trying to launch and grow a multisite church.

COMMUNITY ENGAGEMENT

Attempting to establish a church campus without engaging in the community inevitably creates problems. It's essential to invest time, provide tangible resources, and build relationships. When a multisite church launches a new location, it must not only communicate with the team who will execute ministry activities, but also needs to engage the people the church intends to reach. A multisite church cannot rely on name brand, facilities, or technology to impact a community. It must invest in relationships within its new community. Love covers a multitude of strategic flaws and makes up for the lack of resources, at least to some extent.

VIDEO VENUES

Although this book is not promoting a specific operational style within multisite, I must address one common style, the video venue, because it has received a lot of criticism.[52] I will look at four frequent objections to video venue, although you're likely to hear others.

1. "A video venue promotes idolatry."

Idolatry is a problem in any setting, but especially in churches. House and Allison explain why some people perceive the use of video in church settings to be such a problem: "Digitizing one preaching pastor and beaming his sermon-bearing image into

multiple locations—throughout the city, the extended metropolitan area, the country, or even the entire world—fosters a cult of
personality." But they go on to explain that in this argument, the
real issue is a matter of the heart and not the church model. [53]

One way to resolve the problem is by ensuring that those who
preach are people of integrity and skill. Detailed guidelines for
church leaders may be found in the Pastoral Epistles (1 Timothy,
2 Timothy, and Titus). Key sections in 1 Timothy 3:1-7 and Titus
1:5-9 promote being above reproach (sober-minded, respectable,
hospitable, etc.) and proven ability in managing one's own house-
hold. The same sections forbid drunkenness, love of money,
conceit, quick temper, and other vices. Scripture leaves no room
for pride or promotion of idolatry, whether in the pulpit or on a
large video screen. These guidelines promote godly, healthy leadership and should be the primary standards for those who lead
and preach within the church.

2. "A video venue devalues the pulpit."

The second objection to a video venue is the belief that it
devalues the pulpit. House and Allison state that "the preaching
is done by a disembodied man on a screen, which some critics
consider an illegitimate means of preaching."[54] Many who object
to video venues insist that the only viable option for preaching
follows the example of God sending His Son, Jesus Christ, in the
flesh to save humanity, and Jesus Christ spoke and performed His
ministry face to face with those He encountered. This sentiment
is echoed in the Apostle Paul's letter to Titus: "But as for you,
teach what accords with sound doctrine. . . . Show yourself in all
respects to be a model of good works, and in your teaching show
integrity, dignity, and sound speech that cannot be condemned"

(Titus 2:1, 7-8 ESV). House and Allison observe, "These and other biblical passages are taken to signify that sermons are to be delivered by pastors who are present physically as they preach."[55]

The rebuttal to this objection can be found in the letters written by the Apostle Paul to the various churches and their leaders. Sydney Greidanus addresses this criticism:

> Paul's letters may also be characterized as long-distance preaching. They were like preaching not only because they addressed the specific needs in early churches but also because they were primarily oral communications. Except for brief conclusions (2 Thess 3:17; Gal 6:11; 1 Cor 16:21; Col 4:18), Paul did not write letters but dictated them to secretaries (amanuenses; cf. Rom 16:22) for the purpose of public reading in the churches. Like preaching, therefore, these letters were a form of oral communication. Moreover, in the Greek letter writing tradition, a letter was a stand-in for the presence (*parausia*) of its author. Since Paul was "unable to be present in person, his letters were a direct substitute, and were to be accorded weight equal to Paul's physical presence" (Doty, 36: cf. 1 Cor 5:3-4; 2 Cor 10:11). Listening to Paul's letters being read, therefore, was the same as hearing Paul himself speak—except that the speaking was long-distance and was committed to writing.[56]

I would assume the preferred method of communication would be face to face; however, Greidanus explains that the Apostle Paul utilized the medium of letters to address people he couldn't speak to in person.

One last side note: In recent months we've seen an exponential increase in online communication due to the COVID pandemic. Those who once thought that in-person teaching and preaching was the only viable medium to communicate the Word of God found themselves forced to take their messaging online if they were to continue their calling to preach the Word. Necessity produced creativity.

3. "A video venue limits pastoral care."

A third objection is that lack of pastoral care is likely at a multisite that uses video. This concern is founded upon an assumption of a campus pastor's role and training (or lack thereof). A response to this objection comes from House and Allison:

> The responsibilities of the campus pastor expose the weakness of a critique commonly made of video multisite churches: they suffer from an inability to provide pastoral care, prayer, loving community, and discipline. In our study of multisite churches, virtually all of them address the concern and are committed to providing the full range of pastoral oversight and church ministry at all their campuses. The fact that the campus pastors do not regularly preach on Sundays does not mean they are inactive or unable to provide pastoral care and support in other ways. On the contrary, the campus pastors of who we are aware frequently work with a team of staff and volunteers to exercise leadership in counseling, community group development, children's ministries, youth ministries, outreach, prayer, mercy ministries, church discipline, and other ministries of the church. Also, the

resources available at each campus are potentially available for other campuses to use if needed. This sharing of
resources reflects the strong collaboration desired and
envisioned by multisite churches.[57]

This response highlights the broader scope of the role and
duties this position plays in a multisite church model. Through
my pastoral experience, I've discovered many of a pastor's duties
are fulfilled outside the pulpit. Many pastors experience burnout
from high expectations to perform with excellence in the pulpit
in addition to daily ministry, a multitude of meetings, planning,
preparation, pastoral care, and family life. In a multisite model,
the collaboration between campuses can ensure that each community receives pastoral care even when a campus pastor may
be absent due to vacation, sickness, or various responsibilities.
Additional resources may be shifted from one location to another
to fill the absence, which can alleviate pastoral burnout or the
temporary absence of resources.

4. "A video venue creates a gap between the pastor and the congregation."

In other words, some people complain because the preacher
doesn't know each congregant in a personal way, thus creating
a gap.[58] This criticism is predicated upon the assumption that a
pastor can (and should) know every congregant and all the families in an intimate way. However, even if this ideal relationship is
possible for a pastor of a small congregation or one with high rela-
tional and organizational abilities, sustaining this kind of ministry
may be unhealthy.

In addition, those who point to a gap between the pastor communicating through video venue and the congregants often presume a minimal engagement from the campus pastor whose main task is shepherding the people at that location. House and Allison address this issue by noting that "the concerns are really broader concerns about how to effectively care for and discipline members in large churches."[59] If the multisite church isn't healthy and isn't stimulating good habits of care and discipline, it won't survive; however, if there are quality practices of pastoral care and discipline, a healthy church campus may emerge.

The concern about this gap also suggests there can be little to no positive impact through a video venue. Bird disagrees: "What matters, it seems, is not so much that the preacher knows me personally as that the teacher's message is biblically sound, applied in a way I can understand." He expands this thought by using the example of Billy Graham and his telecasts' impact on many people who found faith while watching him preach.[60] In Billy Graham's telecast and multisite video venues, it's logical to assume the preaching will have a positive impact if the message is biblically sound and understood.

Congregants' questions should be expected and welcomed in every circle of leadership, especially by those leading a multisite church model. Know their objections, wrestle with them, and decide where you stand. You won't be able to win everyone over, but you will be at peace because you've done your homework and you feel confident in your analysis.

Making such decisions before you launch will help you stand strong when you face pushback. I suggest you start with these three:

1. Have I wrestled with these objections to multisite, and am I at peace?

2. Who is on my leadership team who will need help processing these issues?

3. Am I going to set up my multisite to be live preaching or video venue, and why?

CHAPTER 8

THE SCHOOL
OF FAILURE

I was really excited. We had successfully launched our first two campuses, and we were on the way to number three! A respected couple in our church approached me and expressed their burden for the town of Kadoka, South Dakota. At the time, we didn't have the funds to launch another campus. As we discipled this couple's calling and began to train them for this endeavor, I put together a proposal for my denominational district. I presented a vision plan which outlined our goals for this new church campus. When I finished the presentation, I asked our district leaders for enough funds to operate this new location for one year. They agreed, and we were off and running!

As the launch date approached, we faced some hurdles (the politically correct codeword for *problems*) with the campus pastor. He explained that he and his family couldn't move to Kadoka before the launch, so they planned to commute. He also had trouble putting together a launch team until I invested a lot of time on his behalf. Additionally, there were signs that the couple wasn't on the same page . . . publicly or privately. Yet as I observed these yellow and red flags, I minimized them as normal stressors, anxiety, spiritual warfare, and adjusting to a change of career.

The launch day came, and we opened with just over 30 people in the little town of 600. We were already at five percent attendance of the population, including the chief of police. The first few weeks were encouraging and full of life-giving stories, but after about a month, we noticed the attendance starting to dip, and the look on the face of our campus pastor was showing distress. He was having second thoughts and was looking for the exit. Two months later, the couple resigned.

At the time, I had several other people in our leadership pipeline who were being raised up to become pastors, but none of them was ready to leave their careers and start pastoring, nor did they carry a burden for Kadoka. After considering the driving distance and the absence of a pastor, I made the painful decision to close the campus. I felt like a baby had died! There have only been a handful of times in my ministry that I felt this level of pain and failure. It sent me into a spiral of panic and despair. What would people say about me and my church? How would this affect my leadership? Would we ever plant another church again? What about the money the donors gave for this church? Would we abandon the vision God asked us to pursue?

In an attempt to control my fears, I began to write the lessons I was learning from our failure. If we could "fail forward," as John Maxwell likes to say, then we could avoid similar problems in the future. I shared my thoughts with my elders and our district leaders who had donated the funds for this new church campus.

Here were some of the lessons learned:

- The campus pastor makes or breaks a multisite campus, especially a rural multisite. Finding a replacement campus pastor in an urban or suburban setting is much easier than finding a replacement for a town of 600 on the plains of South Dakota.

- Our vetting process was weak. It was mostly based on what I thought I knew about the person. In this case, I knew the campus pastor for two years while he attended our church, and I really liked him. I thought that was good enough. It wasn't. We decided to fix this problem by using a DiSC assessment, an emotional intelligence assessment, and a leadership assessment. Additionally, prospective campus pastors had to attend training and complete assignments through our denomination's church planting arm (Church Multiplication Network [CMN]).

- At the time of this third campus failure, we only required that a rising pastor start and manage a small group, but we realized that wasn't enough training to lead a congregation. We added the requirement of managing and developing a ministry department by creating a successful volunteer base.

- The campus pastor had to have skin in the game before the launch of a church campus. This included several things: The campus pastor had to raise $5,000 to $10,000 outside our church for the support of the campus, and he (or they) had to move to the community before we would advertise the launch of the campus.

These lessons may seem simple (and obvious), but they often aren't. We don't just need well-intentioned volunteers to serve. The church needs men and women who are called, equipped, and ready to shed blood, sweat, and tears for the souls of a community. A well-vetted leader who has skin in the game, carries a true pastoral calling, and has a teachable heart can take any land for the cause of Christ!

This school of failure was harsh, but it shaped our future. As I presented these lessons and what we would do moving forward, my elders boldly asked, "Where are we going to plant next, Pastor?" Our financial donors said, "Thank you for sharing what you've learned. Keep the funds and use them for your next location!"

I felt like I'd gotten a "Get out of jail free" card.

CHAPTER 9

THE GLOVES ARE OFF

When you take the courageous step of expanding the church's vision, watch out! The gloves often come off! Paul wrote at the end of his letter to the Ephesians, "For we do not wrestle against flesh and blood, but against the rulers, against the authorities, against the cosmic powers over this present darkness, against the spiritual forces of evil in the heavenly places" (Ephesians 6:12). Church planting changed the way I view this passage.

I always knew that our battle was not against flesh and blood, but this assumption was tested when we planted churches. During those stressful times, my prayer life shifted because I was often confused about the direction we should take. My confusion prompted me to trust God more than ever. I think that's exactly where God wanted me and where He wants all of us—to come to the end of our abilities and enter into a deeper relationship through prayer. When we think of spiritual warfare, we often look outside the church to see what attack may be coming, but if the enemy can't get you from the outside or through a personal sin, he'll try and take you down from the inside.

As we began to go public with our vision, staff members started getting sick. Several were seeking medical help, only to find their doctors scratching their heads. Several people on the team got sick, and we struggled to understand the causes or find the solutions for their recovery.

One staff member, our children's pastor, found herself with unexplainable physical issues and underwent extensive testing. Finally, over a period of months, the doctors discovered that her body was attacking itself, and she needed regular treatments. Every step of the way, she called her struggle what it was—spiritual warfare. Through her entire ordeal, her testimony was always an encouragement to me.

Later in our church planting campaign, our main campus pastor fell under the weight of some furniture he was moving. He was sore, but his injury didn't appear serious. As time passed, however, he began to lose feeling in his leg and side. One day when we were taking our new campus pastors to the Church Multiplication Network's church plant training in Minneapolis, he was getting out of the van when his leg collapsed and he fell to the ground. During the following weeks, his symptoms worsened to the point where he couldn't walk or control one side of his body. Eventually, the doctors discovered that his C4 vertebra had swollen around his spinal cord, cutting off the nerve. He was rushed to our local medical facility for surgery. His doctors told him the surgery would halt the pain, but it wouldn't improve his numbness and lack of muscle control. They said the operation would keep him out of a wheelchair, but that was about all he could expect. The devil took his gloves off in the season of Kingdom expansion, so we took our gloves off too! Our church rallied around him in prayer. Staff members and congregants called for prayer and fasting. To the testimony of God's power, within 24 hours of his surgery, he was walking again! The doctors said that his recovery was miraculous!

As we planned, prepared, and launched additional campuses, I was more than a little preoccupied. It took me a while—along with some painful conversations—to realize that I'd been missing some important moments with people in our church. For instance, I found out after the fact that a couple was suffering because the husband had been diagnosed with heart disease. I knew them well, but somehow, I didn't hear the bad news until weeks after they got the diagnosis. They wondered if I still cared.

Babies were born, kids graduated from high school, people fell in love, and a few couples decided to call it quits. Before I got involved in multisite, I paid more attention and got more involved. I'd been present with people—body, soul, and spirit— as they went through pleasant or painful transitions, but during these launches, my radio wasn't dialed to the right frequency. Something had to change.

The lesson is clear: No matter what tasks are ahead of you, don't lose sight of the fact that the church and church planting is about people. If you're very task-driven like me, stop and remind yourself of the people God has entrusted to you.

Throughout this season, several church members walked away because they felt we shouldn't put our time and resources into other communities. They voiced their frustration as we raised funds for new church plants in underserved areas. We also challenged the congregation to deploy their gifts in serving these new campuses to help them get on their feet. Sometimes I wonder if the discomfort of a call to engagement frustrates the Pharisee in each of us. If you're a pastor or church leader, you've undoubtedly had people leave for one reason or another. The hard part is not taking it personally. I'm still working on this skill! But if I take a step back and remind myself of Ephesians 6:12, I'll put my efforts in the right place—prayer!

I hate conflict. I avoid it at every turn, but sometimes it finds me, bites me, and won't let go. During our season of church planting, I stayed very busy. I was dealing with many legitimate obstacles that prevented me from spending as much time with people as I would have liked, but in retrospect, those seem like lame excuses. During this time, one couple in our church got very upset with me. As I was being pulled in several directions managing seven church plants, leading additional staff and campus pastors, and trying to pastor a growing congregation, their daughter had been hospitalized with a disease, and I couldn't visit her. They interpreted my absence as "Pastor Gerad doesn't care about us." I discovered their resentment the hard way: they complained to a lot of people until the word finally got around to me. By the time I called to meet with them, their daughter was out of the hospital and recovering. I asked if I could visit them at their home, and we sat on their porch for a long talk. I asked them to forgive me for not being more attentive. I admitted that I could have at least called them when their daughter was in the hospital, and I assured them that I really care about them. At the end, I prayed for them and we hugged. It was just what we all needed.

I could tell you a lot more stories, but you get the drift. I've asked myself countless times what I could have done differently in each difficult situation. I certainly made some mistakes and had my share of blind spots, but I've learned many lessons from those moments. I've seen patterns in how people behave and how the enemy uses their painful situations to try to derail leaders and churches. But I've also learned that our behavior and vision can be sharpened and moved forward when we're on our knees in prayer.

The task of expanding God's kingdom isn't a casual walk. Leading can be very intense. During our two-year vision plan where we went from one to seven church locations, I had many sleepless nights and countless moments when I wanted to quit. From staff sicknesses and angry congregants to hate-mail and betrayal, the enemy took his gloves off, trying to discourage and derail the vision God had placed in our hearts. However, I remembered what God assigned me to do: plant campuses and own our region. My prayer life grew, and if you start on this journey, yours will too! In fact, God will use any difficulties to deepen your faith and make you a better leader . . . all while reaching the lost and the least in other rural communities.

CHAPTER 10

CHANGE STARTS WITH ME

The first pastor I served under, Alan Bixler, taught me a very simple concept I often remind myself of: When we read the Scriptures and apply them, we need to ask, "Is this a principle or a preference?" For instance, Jesus said, "I am the way and the truth and the life. No one comes to the Father except through me" (John 14:6). That's a biblical principle, and we are expected to change our lives to conform to God's principles.

On the other hand, much of church life comes down to personal preference: "The choruses we're singing aren't worship" (so we need to change), or "We can't move to two services because we won't know everyone" (so we *shouldn't* change). How are church leaders to respond to such comments?

Change is inevitable, but it becomes easier to handle after you determine if a decision is based on a principle or a preference. Difficult conversations about vision, strategy, and practice become manageable when the leader begins to change the way people think about the differences between unchanging principles and preferences that may seem immutable but aren't.

Even when we realize change has to happen, we often don't know where to start. Our process of renewal began with one of my mentors, Rick Allen, coaching me through the "Acts 2 Journey," created and taught by Alton Garrison, the assistant general superintendent of the Assemblies of God. This process poses ten crucial questions related to mission, vision, values, planning, and implementation. We used it to analyze our current status and plan effectively for the future. It's easy to point the finger at music or programs that need to be updated (or eliminated), but I've discovered that the most significant change that needed to be addressed wasn't in the services or ministries, or even the congregation. It had to start with me!

DEVELOPING LEADERS

Pastoring the church through renewal required me to think differently. As the leader, I needed to change the way I recruited leaders and volunteers. One of the pleasures of my pastoral responsibility is "to equip the saints for the work of the ministry"—to involve, train, and place others where they can see God use them. This perspective is critical if you want to multiply. As renewal begins and the church grows, you'll need to recruit higher capacity volunteers and staff.

As we considered hiring staff members and finding key volunteers, we focused on the future vision for our church, the core values of our leadership, and the strategic plan that would lead us toward renewal. Rick Allen said something that hit me like a brick: "You like to 'pick up puppies on the side of the road.'" He didn't mean it as a compliment. I thought it was a strength to always see potential in people, but Rick showed me that I needed to be shrewd as well as kind. It was a hard lesson, but one that was crucial, especially as we expanded to new campuses and needed high capacity staff members who could serve with excellence.

Don't get me wrong, I've seen young believers become incredible leaders with the proper time and mentorship. But as I began to grow as a pastor, I learned to look for those who had been faithful in the little things and were already proving their leadership abilities. I truly believe our church has grown because we've opened the doors for our people to step up and serve, and the leadership pipeline has expanded from a trickle to a torrent!

SELF-AWARENESS

I've also learned to be far more self-aware—not self-absorbed, but aware of my skills and my limitations—and especially, to know what I don't know. I knew we needed change, but I didn't always know how to bring it about. I found it's necessary to ask the right question, directed toward the right person, at the right time. King Solomon instructs us:

> My son, if you receive my words and treasure up my commandments with you, making your ear attentive to wisdom and inclining your heart to understanding; yes,

if you call out for insight and raise your voice for understanding, if you seek it like silver and search for it as for
hidden treasures, then you will understand the fear of the
Lord and find the knowledge of God. (Proverbs 2:1-5
ESV)

I was able to change only because I sought out the wisdom of
those who took the time to answer my questions and pushed me
to grow. I learned how to build healthy relationships that enable
people to find their purpose in ministry and leadership. I learned
how to give people room to grow instead of boxing them in by the
rules of the church or my expectations.

CRUCIAL QUESTIONS

Let's look at a few of the questions that may help turn a church
toward renewal.

How do I keep people from leaving the church?

Every pastor who experiences someone walking out the door
feels this pain. It feels personal, and in some cases, it is. However,
it might sometimes be the pruning of a zealous leader who needs
to grow in wisdom. Over time, God has shown me who I am as
a leader and who we are as a church. When that was solidified, I
began to operate by a revolutionary thought: "We need to choose
who we will lose so we can choose who we will gain." This statement isn't narrow, harsh, or judgmental . . . just true.

My new perspective relieved the pressure when people left
the church who weren't in alignment with our vision. I would
rather someone leave and thrive somewhere else than stay and be
miserable. Every church is only a generation away from closing its

doors—a realization that has motivated many of our decisions. We knew we wanted to be a multigenerational church, so renewal required us to focus our efforts toward the next generation. Our slogan is, "Honor the past but prepare for the future." We know our church won't be a fit for everyone, and I'm good with that . . . but it took a change of thinking to get us (that's code for *me*) to that point.

Is culture the same as vision?

In our purpose statement, we articulated our vision very clearly. We knew what we wanted people to experience when they walked through our doors. We wore wristbands to remind us, wrote it on the walls, and included it on our letterhead. However, we quickly learned that words are sterile until they align with behavior and atmosphere.

Bryan Jarrett, pastor of North Place Church in Dallas, Texas, shared a succinct sentence with me: "Culture is more powerful than vision." This statement has become a staple on our leadership team. *Vision* is what we want people to know about our church; *culture* is how they feel when they're with us. When a church confirms its vision and understands its culture, the leaders can create powerful moments that will change people's lives. When visionary words are paired with loving behavior and a welcoming atmosphere, God does the impossible!

How do I change the culture?

The simple and profound answer is: "You get what you celebrate!" The church and its people are often quick to tell others what's wrong, sinful, and unholy. Too often, we're known for what we're against rather than what we're for. Consequently, Christians are often labeled by the world as bigots, haters, and hypocrites, but we can change that perception by changing our hearts and how we treat others. Jesus told His disciples, "A new commandment I give to you, that you love one another: just as I have loved you, you also are to love one another. By this all people will know that you are my disciples, if you have love for one another" (John 13:34-35 ESV).

The concept of "You get what you celebrate" shifts our attitudes and changes our behavior. In a very simple but effective fix, we began to share with our community what we're for. We want to be a hospital for the sick to come and experience the Healer! We want to lead people to the Way if they're lost! We want our church to be a place of worship and celebration for the King of kings! That's why, after every altar call, we rejoice and applaud. We celebrate, and it never gets old. We remind our people of the prodigal's father's explanation of why he threw a party when his son returned home: "It was fitting to celebrate and be glad, for this your brother was dead, and is alive; he was lost, and is found" (Luke 15:32 ESV). We're learning that the power of celebration encourages our people to replicate the principles of Scripture.

A healthy culture is also a result of a clear calling. Changing culture can only happen if it starts from the top and trickles down to the rest of the leadership, and then to the congregation. This requires change from the senior pastor, and then the board, ministry teams, and ministry leaders. Each of us is called first to the Lord, then to our body of believers, and then to our area of service. For instance, board members need to be careful that they operate through a biblical perspective. During their orientation, we want our new board members to sense their God-given calling so they see their role as much more than an organizational manager or representative for their friends in the congregation. Sometimes, they'll be called to make hard decisions their friends won't like! Our board members aren't politicians who are angling for support; they're spiritual elders charged with leading God's people with integrity and love. When our board members realize they represent the vision of the church to the people, hearts begin to change, and our culture begins to improve.

Are we healthy?

As I mentioned earlier, I once heard that a healthy church should regularly see salvations and water baptisms. We know this is foundational to the purpose of the church, but it can also feel like an impossible mission. We rarely saw these healthy markers, so we began to change how we went about pursuing them. Celebrating healthy markers like salvation and water baptisms reinforced another principle: We need to "measure what matters." Attendance matters because each number is a soul. Guest retention matters because we needed to know if they felt welcomed into the family. You get the idea. As we began to measure what matters, we were able to have incredible celebrations, but we also found that areas of our ministry needed more focused attention. For example, we noticed little attention had been placed on Holy Spirit baptism. We had to change that! Through measuring what matters, we've begun to provide special ministry services focused on the nature and work of the Holy Spirit.

Evaluating the church can be a painful and sobering process, but measuring will inevitably reveal well-intentioned ministry that's no longer bearing fruit. These revelations become launching pads for healthy change.

How do I kill something? (You're about to see this is the wrong question!)

Styles of ministries are simply tools to accomplish the Great Commission; however, tools eventually wear out, requiring them to be replaced. I learned very quickly that throwing away or "killing" these tools implied a lack of respect. Those tools once brought value, life change, and hope, and in fact, every tool was connected to some individual. If I killed a tool, I was undoubtedly hurting someone.

When a church is in the renewal process, some of their tools need to be replaced. How do we make needed changes without offending people? Rick Allen reminded me that every tool deserves the respect of a beautiful "sunset," which precedes the magnificent sunrise of something new and relevant. People need respect and time before they can let go of the previous tool and grab hold of the new. Sunsets are always followed by sunrises. The sunset may bring a moment of pain, but Scripture promises: "Weeping may tarry for the night, but joy comes in the morning" (Psalm 30:5). The sunrise creates hope and promises a better future.

Let me give an example: Our church operated a community outreach for almost nine years called "Wednesday Night Club." We bused neighborhood kids to our church for dinner, activities, and Bible lessons. When it started, this ministry was revolutionary for Bethel. It shifted the mindset of the church from inward- to outward-focused and challenged our congregants to volunteer and engage in hands-on ministry. (Notice how I'm honoring the past? If you can't honor the past, people won't dream with you for the future. Now back to the story.)

We planted seeds of salvation into countless kids over the years, and we showed parents in our neighborhood we were a safe place for their children. Over time, though, this ministry became stagnant and exhausting. We stubbornly continued to consider it a success, but only because we were keeping it going, not because it was changing a lot of lives. When we finally admitted that the volunteers were not really excited or engaged in this ministry and that it was no longer bringing new families into the church, we realized we needed a better definition of *success*. It was time to give the Wednesday Night Club program a sunset.

To replace this once-valuable tool, we were determined to give our volunteers and our congregation a new tool to reach the kids in our community. It took time, it caused some heartache, and it required a healthy dose of creativity, but the result was worth the effort.

Our sunrise was the adoption of an elementary school in our neighborhood. We pursued the same kids, but in a different way. We built a relationship with the school and began to serve them without any strings attached. We honor the teachers and staff by catering lunch for them during pre-service and providing snacks for the lounge a few times a month. We place volunteers in and around the building on orientation nights to help parents find their children's classrooms and teachers. In addition, Bethel volunteers are in the classrooms each week mentoring kids in math and reading. Every year we partner with the school to provide a bicycle for any child who has had perfect attendance. The first year the school only needed 12 bikes, but last year, they needed 53. Praise God!! Through this new partnership with the school, we've seen families and staff of the school enter the doors of our church! It is a new tool with the same purpose, sharing the light of Jesus in a dark world.

Some of you reading this book are pastors and board members of established churches, and you're considering adding locations in a rural context. If your story turns out to be anything like mine, get ready, because change is coming!

Change has been possible because of the men and women who call Bethel their home. Although the renewal process was gut-wrenching, it was entirely worth every disappointment and difficulty because it changed lives. Bethel ultimately grew to a congregation worshiping at seven locations! We moved from a plateaued church to a multiplying church that's committed to see not just the community but the entire region discover Jesus Christ! Our vision echoes the heart of the Church Multiplication Network, "A healthy church in every community," by investing in the rural places of our region.

STAGES OF CHANGE

For pastors and other church leaders who are considering the multisite model in rural areas, change is a constant companion. I've learned a few things as we've expanded from a single campus to seven. I still have a lot to learn, but let me outline the stages we and other multisite churches have gone through.

Welcome discontent.

A sense of unease may be the residual effect of the hot wings you had last night, but it could also be the Spirit of God prompting you to see what you haven't seen before. Things aren't always the way they *should* be or what they *can* be. Consequently, discontent almost always accompanies the first stage in receiving a new vision and crafting a new strategy. Don't assume a time of confusion and anxiety is a sign you're not walking with the

Lord. He may be shaking up your status quo and preparing you for greater things.

Do the hard work of analysis.

A time of rigorous evaluation is absolutely necessary. Take a long, hard look at your leadership development strategy and success. Are you raising up enough leaders to expand your own church? Are you raising up enough people to plant a church in a nearby community? What are the open doors? Where are people longing for you to come and be a presence for Christ? Take out a map and do some demographic analysis to determine what towns don't have churches like yours. Where is the need? Where are the opportunities? Where is God leading? Those aren't easy questions with simple solutions. Struggle with these questions until you have reasonable answers and clear direction.

Learn to live with a measure of ambiguity.

Most of us don't like ambiguity. We want clarity, and we want it now! I've learned, though, that answers to the hard questions seldom surface quickly. I've had to let the process play out over time and become more comfortable saying, "I'm not sure. We'll keep studying and praying until we have an answer." When the lights come on, you'll know it.

Get input from trusted sources.

God has provided some wonderful people and organizations to help as you consider and take steps to implement a multisite model. CMN is a treasure, and plenty of pastors who have been successful are happy to talk to you. I would suggest, though, that you find a mentor to coach you through the process. That person will become a great comfort when you're struggling and a source of wisdom to guide the way. I have had a few mentors, and each of them has played a key role shaping my ministry, but more importantly, in shaping me.

Plan exhaustively.

Some of us are naturally good at the planning process, and others shoot from the hip. I can tell you that those in the second category are in for big trouble if they don't develop some planning expertise! Murphy's Law runs rampant in multisite: if anything can go wrong, it will! I would normally advise leaders to avoid being obsessive, but in this case, it's wise to take time to think through as many contingencies as possible. Make sure you focus on selecting and developing leaders who share your heart and vision for the community where the church will be launched, and build in lead time to structure a team, gather resources, and promote the launch. Rushing things inevitably produces anxiety and regrets.

Gather resources.

Church planting organizations can provide a detailed catalog of what it takes to launch a campus, including funding, personnel, equipment, promotional materials, timelines, and everything else you'll need. Such complex plans seldom come together quickly, so expect a few delays along the way to great victories.

Take the step.

After all the analysis, planning, equipping, and gathering of resources, at some point it's time to take the bold step: set a date. Rent the facilities, promote the launch, prepare the team, and show up to see what God will do.

Care for the baby.

As all new parents know, the moment of birth isn't the end of the process; it's only the beginning. Some launch teams are so exhausted by the first service that they need to take a break for a few weeks. That doesn't work! Reserve enough energy and do enough planning so everyone on the team is prepared to keep loving, serving, and giving for weeks and months after the launch.

Keep developing leaders.

It was crucial to develop leaders for the launch, and it's just as important to keep developing leaders as the new plant is established. Yes, you want to do outreach. Yes, you need to organize and prepare programs. But in everything you do, keep an eye on developing the people on your team (and the people on their teams), not just on having successful events. Your new church will flourish to the extent that you see God raise up "workers for the harvest."

A FEW FINAL REMINDERS

Throughout this process, simple but profound leadership principles can be applied. Let me list a few to keep in mind.

- Change always includes losses and gains, grief and celebration. Value both sides.

- During seasons of change, people take decisions personally because they are affected personally. Don't be surprised by their reactions of fear or anger.

- Everyone accepts change at their own pace. Very few people will adopt the changes right away. Most will need more questions answered before they are willing to buy in. They're not evil for being a bit slower. It's your job to bring them along.

- Don't pressure people to conform. Instead, invite them into the adventure.

- If you're anxious, they'll be anxious. If you're calm and confident, they'll be reassured.

- Invest in the process of change more than the change itself. That means it's important to focus on communication, resources, and timing.

Leaders have different personalities and different strengths. There's not a universal "multisite pastor's profile." If you have a heart for God and for lost people, God will use your unique personality and talents to craft a plan, raise up gifted and passionate workers, and reach people who would never drive to visit your home church.

CHAPTER 12

NUTS AND BOLTS

P astors often ask me for "the nuts and bolts" of launching a new campus. That's what this chapter is about. Below is a succinct summary of most of the important matters.

ROLLING OUT THE VISION

Plant Seeds

- Share your burden with your spouse and a trusted friend.

- Share your vision with an early adopter on your elder or deacon board.

- Share your vision with influential leaders in your church whom you know to be early adopters.

- Gather two or three leaders who are late adopters, but who can be trusted. Share with them the vision and listen intently to their questions, objections, and fears. Don't move on to the next step until you have adequately wrestled with these leaders' issues. (That doesn't mean you've sold them on the vision, but it does mean they feel heard and understood.)

- Begin to incorporate imaginative movements of God in people's lives outside of your community. These are "I-have-a-dream" type moments.

Call out future leaders of the church

- Begin to look at influencers, leaders, and volunteers with spiritual eyes. Watch for saints who are waiting for you to see greater things in them! And don't forget your responsibility as a pastor "to equip the saints for the work of ministry, for building up the body of Christ."

- Remember that God can do amazing things as you lead the church and care for the people God entrusts to you. A young military man in our community found out his wife had been unfaithful, and he felt crushed. One day, as he pointed his loaded pistol at his head, he saw a commercial for our church on TV and suddenly felt that he should put the gun down and give the church a try. He walked into our morning service that Sunday and gave his life to Jesus. A few weeks later he walked into the church with his wife, and she then gave her life to Jesus. Fast forward several years: he became one of our new rural campus pastors!

Create moments to call people toward greater things.

- We started a Leadership Academy to provide cohort-style learning. We read, discuss, and teach using books on leadership, pastoral care, and spiritual development. From this cohort came some of our future pastors and key leaders.

- We also started "The Shepherd's Table" where I invited people whom I believed had a call on their lives to join me every other week for morning coffee before they went to work. We discussed what it's like to be a pastor. I corrected any common misassumptions about what many perceive about the glitz or glamour of leading a church and shared what I call "the backside of ministry." I reminded them that people are messy and assured them that being a pastor who's involved in people's lives is quite stressful. If the participants don't step into ministry, they at least become sympathetic leaders in the church who have a greater understanding of what pastors go through. They become armor bearers and champions of clergy!

- Beyond the development of a healthy church culture, it's the people who are the carriers of the vision. Without a rider, your horse won't even begin a journey. Invest in people! Invest in leaders!

Call for the question.

- When you've adequately planted seeds in key leaders and influencers of your board and church, you can begin to place deliberate discussion items on your board agenda.

- After your leadership has adopted the burden, you're ready to declare the vision to the congregation.

DEVELOP A VISION PLAN

Do your research.

- What are the demographics of where you're going to plant?

- What is the need of the community? Discover the need and determine if your ministry can meet that need in a tangible way.

- If you can meet the need, connect that need to a story and use it in your vision plan. Be prepared to answer others' questions:

  Why? If people know why you're doing something, they will often support it. This is where your research comes in. Articulate *why* your church needs to carry the burden.

  What? Describe what your church will do to meet the burden and how it will be done through planting campuses. Describe where you will go, the opportunities that are waiting, and how your new campus will become a permanent part of your church family and network.

  How? Describe the phases of the process that will help leaders and donors understand how the vision will be accomplished. Identify the campus pastor (the rider for the horse) and the planned location of the campus. Explain whether the campus will have live preaching or be a video venue.

Formulate your budget.

- Give an overview of the budget to operate the campus. My personal philosophy on financial support of a rural campus is based on an observation by Ed Stetzer: "If a church is not financially viable within four years, it probably never will be." Therefore, we challenge our rural campuses to move toward financial viability within four years. The first year, we provide 100 percent support; the second year, 75 percent; the third year, 50 percent; and the fourth year, 25 percent. As our support gradually scales back, it gives our campus pastors time to get on their feet, establish a congregation, and begin to promote the principle of giving (tithing). It also allows each pastor and congregation to develop a level of ownership in their church.

- The geographical location of the church will affect its financial obligations, but for illustration purposes, consider this as a basic rural campus budget:

Campus Pastor Salary: $25,000 (bi-vocational)

Facilities (monthly): $12,000 ($1k per month)

Equipment (AV, Kids, etc.): $35,000 (one-time expense)

Outreach: $12,000

Advertising: $8,000

- In a rural setting, relationships are key. A bi-vocational pastor can more smoothly integrate into the community and build trust in relationships. Although I was the lead pastor of a multisite church and didn't need the additional income, I served our county Sheriff's Office as the head chaplain and reserve deputy. This role gave me greater insight into our community and allowed me to build relationships outside the church walls. And I loved every minute of it! (I sometimes told people who had gotten in trouble, "I could arrest you and then pray for you!")

- Create a timeline of key events, fundraisers, and potential goals for planting the church campus.

- The goal for the vision plan is to create an all-encompassing document of these items (and possibly more) to present to key donors, church leaders, and potential campus pastors. This document should be treated as a living vision plan. In other words, it can be adjusted as new information surfaces. In the end, it provides a roadmap for you and your leadership team.

- You and your leadership may decide to establish some locations as a missional endeavor because they're important, even though you know they'll never be financially viable. For example, one of our campuses was located at a homeless shelter. From the beginning, we determined it would be a missional endeavor, and that was okay.

Move your leaders and ministries toward a multisite mindset.

- Daily, weekly, and monthly conversations should include casting vision. Don't limit your focus to your ministry's current needs, but expand your concern and your service to other locations.

- When you begin to sense that other people are sick of hearing about your plans and can repeat everything you are saying, you're just getting to the point where they're beginning to understand. Don't stop now!

Raise up leaders who can help at another location temporarily or permanently.

- Understand that "the people who got you here, won't always get you there." Not everyone's capacity can fulfill greater expectations; therefore, you need to determine if people are in the wrong seat on the bus . . . or if they're on the wrong bus.

Set goals for your leaders/departments in preparation for launching another campus.

- For example, have your Children's Pastor develop curriculum and training for the volunteers of the new campus. Set deadlines to order check-in systems, nursery supplies, and kids' church supplies.

Other important questions to ask:

- Who are my key influencers?

- Within my key influencers, who are my early adopters?

- Who are my late adopters?

- Do we have the financial ability to launch another campus, or do we need to raise funds?

- Has God given me a timeline to execute this vision?

- Do I have the right people on the bus? Do I need to move people's seats on the bus?

CHAPTER 13

SUCCESSION

When I was an associate pastor, my Lead Pastor confided that he was sensing a different calling and asked me if I would be willing to replace him at Bethel. I was overwhelmed with the honor, yet he and I quickly found ourselves in the uncharted waters of pastoral succession. Most businesses realize that carefully anticipated, planned, and executed succession is a sign of organizational health, but in rural church leadership, succession has been largely ignored. My Lead Pastor and I developed a succession plan to ensure a smooth transfer of authority, and later, when I moved on to the next assignment God had for me, the church followed a similar plan and process. The plans differed in some respects because the situations were different, so in this chapter I'll discuss both.

BECOMING THE LEAD PASTOR

My Lead Pastor, Jim Sorum, is a rare leader. He wasn't threatened by the process of releasing his church to a younger minister.

In fact, he welcomed the endeavor and helped me to gradually grow into the role. In addition, we brought in a consultant, Rick Allen, whom I have mentioned before, to help us shape the strategy. He helped Jim and me stay on track and resolve any differences in our leadership styles. I'm forever indebted to both Jim and Rick for their gracious attitudes and their confidence in me. As you begin the process of succession, both the Lead Pastor and the successor must have clear communication, a foundation of trust, and full transparency.

Our strategy began behind closed doors with the board of elders. We first needed to ensure each elder was on board and willing to walk out the process. With their blessing, Jim and I met regularly with our consultant over a nine-month period as he helped us see blind spots and kept us on the right path. I had much to learn. As associate pastor, I hadn't been familiar with all the internal workings of the church (board meetings, budgets, church influencers, etc.), nor had I regularly filled the pulpit. I needed to be brought into those processes.

Working together, here is the succession plan we created.

KEY STEPS TO SUCCESSION

1. The successor needs to attend all board meetings and help shape each board agenda (at the invitation of the current Lead Pastor). The board needs to begin to see the successor in a business leadership role and allow for wins and mistakes.

2. The Lead Pastor and successor work together to shape the annual budget. The budget will often reflect the heart of the pastor, and this is a critical step to allow the successor to begin grafting his heart into the budgetary process.

3. The Lead Pastor and successor need to work together on the pulpit strategy. Not only do they shape content together, but also regularly rotate preaching in the pulpit to establish familiarity and trust with the congregation. Strategically select weekends where both the Lead Pastor and successor tag-team preach. This approach helps the congregation see the trust of the two leaders as well as the potential of the successor.

4. The Lead Pastor and successor, along with the consultant (if possible), onboard the staff and key leaders, presenting the approved succession plan. Allow a window of time for questions, concerns and feedback. Notice a "window of time" because the leadership have already made their decision. This is not up for debate.

5. The Lead Pastor makes the succession plan public and champions the successor. From this point, there should be a clear plan established and presented based on the church governance.

6. The newly established Lead Pastor should honor the past and the Lead Pastor who had the vision for succession. The previous Lead Pastor should honor the new Lead Pastor, both publicly and privately championing the vision of the future.

You can find plenty of excellent books, articles, and blogs on succession; however, very few are specifically about rural churches. The next generation needs leaders like Jim Sorum who look toward the future to hand their ministries off to the next generation!

PASSING THE MANTLE

Years later, when our seven campuses were in full swing, I found myself in the back of our auditorium during a staff chapel experience. I was praying and journaling. I had been seeking the Lord through prayer and fasting, looking for direction for the next season. In that moment, I felt an overwhelming feeling that I needed to write this question: "God, are You done with me here? Have I completed the assignment You set out for me to accomplish?" Later that day, I received a call from a friend asking me to consider joining his team to help with multisite and a rural pastors network called the "Water Tower Network." As soon as he said it, I knew that was my next assignment.

I had already been preparing our main campus pastor to become a Lead Pastor. (He was the pastor I mentioned in Chapter 9 who had almost lost total mobility and was miraculously restored after his surgery.) He had indicated months before that he felt God leading him to become a Lead Pastor someday, so I had immediately begun preparing him for the weight and responsibility of sitting in the lead seat of another church somewhere in America.

After receiving the call from my friend to join his team in Texas, I realized that all the time and training I had been pouring into my main campus pastor was preparing him to become my successor. Following a time of prayer, conversation with my wife, and seeking godly council, I asked him to consider becoming the Lead Pastor of Bethel. He agreed, and we began the official process of passing the mantle.

The intricacies of succession will be determined by the church's bylaws (church governance). In our case, I needed to seek the approval of the board of elders and ask them to consider our main campus pastor as the primary candidate to be presented to the members of the church. With that approval, we could to go public with my resignation and announce a clear plan of succession.

He was already attending my board meetings, so I started having him lead the board agendas and learn Robert's Rules of Order—something they never teach you in Bible college! Additionally, I explained to him our church bylaws, staff development, and key church leader engagement. I increased his pulpit exposure by having him speak regularly, not only at our main campus, but at all our campuses. He began to lead our staff meetings. This increased exposure bolstered his leadership and experience while allowing me to step away to work on a fresh vision for the church.

A word of caution: Don't leave your successor in the dark on critical areas just because you were left in the dark as a new leader. Don't think to yourself, *I was never taught how to manage a church board, lead a staff, balance a budget, or cast vision, so he can figure it out on his own.* That's not the heart of a Paul and Timothy relationship!

Passing the mantle needs to be rooted in our own identity and security. I learned this clearly from Jim Sorum. Succession will only be successful when you're comfortable with your own leadership. We don't need more King Sauls holding on to their kingdoms longer than they should, throwing spears, and threatening young King Davids (1 Samuel 18—19)!

If you are a Lead Pastor who is led to move to another ministry, and you want to leave your beloved church in the capable hands of a qualified and prepared successor, below are some guidelines that may be quite helpful.

WORKING YOURSELF OUT OF A JOB

- *Identify talented leaders and raise them up*. Spend time with your leaders, and let them get their hands dirty in various levels of leadership. Don't do all the work yourself. A good rule of thumb is that if they can do a task at 80 percent of your ability, then let them do it.

- *Lead with an open hand*. Don't clinch your fist and hold (control) leaders too tightly. If you keep your hand open, God can take anyone He wants from your hand, and He can also place anyone He wants into your hand. Build people up to replace you, but if God should move them to another assignment, be thankful you've participated in expanding God's greater kingdom!

- *Build trust and increase responsibility*. Give your talented leaders a greater level of responsibility. If they fail (and they will), show them the mistake, coach them toward the proper action, and then let them try again. Discipleship isn't just about Bible studies and theology; it's also about raising up leaders in the body of Christ and preparing them for their God-given assignments, which include the management of bodies, budgets, and buildings.

- *Seek feedback*. Ask for input from your leaders, and also from the people under them. Too often, pastors don't value feedback loops. We need to understand how our leaders make people feel, so we need to hear praises and concerns from the people they minister to. This will help you make adjustments in equipping your potential successor.

- *Place the mantle and step away.* The greatest joy (and greatest pain) is turning your ministry over to someone else. You have to trust that you heard from the Lord, walk away, and allow people in the church to trust and follow your successor.

Don't be surprised if you see God's hand in unexpected ways during the succession process. Before we moved our church toward multisite, we had endeavored to update our church's bylaws to be consistent with our plan to have multiple locations. One significant change was revising the bylaws to allow for mail-in voting. This proved to be a timely decision. Two weeks after I announced my resignation and presented our main campus pastor as the candidate to succeed me, our world came to a screeching halt due to the COVID pandemic. The congregation was sad over my announcement, yet also hopeful because they had grown to trust and love our Lead Pastor candidate. However, they needed to approve the change in leadership, and live meetings were on hold indefinitely. By the grace and sovereignty of God, we were able to proceed with the election of my successor because we had changed our bylaws and everyone could vote by mail.

Looking back over the process of preparing my successor, it took time, heart, and intentionality to develop the right person for the role. If you follow these key steps, you'll find yourself surrounded by great leaders on whose shoulders you can place the mantle, and others who will go to other parts of the harvest field to serve faithfully and well.

Look for your successor, pray for God's clear leading, and invest the time to prepare that person, the team, the elders, and the church. The investment will pay big dividends.

CHAPTER 14

WHY THIS?
WHY NOW?

B y this point in the book, you know my heart. You also know many of my strengths and weaknesses as a leader. Let me take these last few paragraphs to summarize my case.

Rural communities are declining. Draw a line across the country in any direction, and it will pass through towns that are only a shadow of what they were before. The reasons are economic and social. People can find better paying jobs in cities and suburbs, and they can live closer to more people and have more services. Drugs used to be a big city problem, but addiction is now a rural catastrophe as well. In addition, farming practices have radically changed, and small farms are almost a thing of the past. The people in small towns feel abandoned and left out of the American dream.

But God hasn't forgotten them. Each person is so valuable to Him that Jesus came to live and die to rescue them from eternal destruction. People in these communities aren't just statistics, faceless numbers on a demographic chart. They're people God dearly loves.

We see these communities as far more than dots on a map. The Great Commission includes every person in every small town, and the Great Commandment motivates us to reach out to them. We are the hands, feet, and voice of Jesus in a lost, lonely, and dying world. We don't have unlimited resources, so we must find creative ways to touch their lives. There may be hundreds of good and viable strategies to reach them, but one I know that really works is the multisite model.

As we think, talk, pray, and plan, we want to reach more people with the gospel, make more disciples in small towns, and strengthen more rural churches. But as we do, we need to remember that the *who* is far more important than the *what*. Our first and most important calling isn't to a ministry model, a denomination, or a particular church. It's to Jesus. When we get that right (and keep it right), we have the inner security to be bold and creative. I'm not really a champion of any ministry model. I'm only a servant of the King, and the King has given me His heart and a vision for people I would never meet in a hundred years.

In his brilliant book, *The Call,* Os Guinness succinctly explains what's primary and what's secondary: "Calling is the truth that God calls us to himself so decisively that everything we are, everything we do, and everything we have is invested with a special devotion and dynamism lived out as a response to his summons and service."[61] Devotion and dynamism . . . that sounds a lot like spiritual renewal, doesn't it? As we answer God's call to put Him first, we'll work hard to expand His kingdom, and we'll consider every opportunity.

Why is the multisite strategy important now? Sure, we can wait a few years or a few decades to see if those little communities stage a comeback, but in the meantime, people need Jesus. They're lost *now*. They're hopeless *now*. They need forgiveness *now*. They need God to give them a far bigger purpose *now*.

God has given me a strong sense of urgency to use our story and the church as a sending center so people in other communities can come to faith and live meaningful lives as children of the Creator, the King, the Savior. That's what this book has been about. That's what my life is about. If you've read this far, I'm quite sure that's what you're about too.

ENDNOTES

1   United States Census Bureau, Rural America, https://www.census.gov/library/stories/2017/08/rural-america.html

2   Kristin Tate, "Americans Leave Large Cities for Suburban Areas and Rural Towns," The Hill, July 5, 2020, https://thehill.com/opinion/finance/505944-americans-leave-large-cities-for-suburban-areas-and-rural-towns

3   Mary Jo Neitz, "Reflections on Religion and Place: Rural Churches and American Religion," *Journal for the Scientific Study of Religion*, 44.3 (2005), p. 244, accessed January 1, 2019.

4   "10 Facts about America's Churchless," Barna Group, December 10, 2014, accessed January 29, 2019, https://www.barna.com/research/10-facts-about-americas-churchless/

5   See Brad House and Gregg Allison, *Multichurch: Exploring the Future of Multisite* (Grand Rapids: Harper Collins Publishers, 2017); Geoff Surratt, Greg Ligon, and Warren Bird, *The Multi-Site Church Revolution: Being One Church . . . in Many Locations* (Grand Rapids: Zondervan, 2006); Geoff Surratt, Greg Ligon, and Warren Bird, *Multi-site Church Road Trip* (Grand Rapids: Zondervan, 2009); Brian Nathaniel Frye, *"The Multi-Site Church Phenomenon in North America: 1950-2010"* (PhD diss., The Southern Baptist Theological Seminary, 2011); Barna Group, "More Than Multisite: Inside Today's Methods and Models for Launching New Congregations" (The Barna Group, 2016); J. D. Greear, "A Pastor Defends His Multi-Site Church," *9 Marks*, February 25, 2010, accessed December 28, 2018, https://www.9marks.org/article/pastor-defends-his-multi-site-church/

6   Geoff Surratt, Greg Ligon, and Warren Bird, *The Multi-Site Church Revolution: Being One Church . . . in Many Locations* (Grand Rapids: Zondervan, 2006), p. 18.

7   A megachurch is a church with an unusually large congregation, typically over 2000 in attendance.

8   Geoff Surratt, Greg Ligon, and Warren Bird, *Multi-site Church Road Trip* (Grand Rapids: Zondervan, 2009), pp. 14-15.

9   United States Census Bureau, "Rural America," https://www.census.gov/library/stories/2017/08/rural-america.html

10 Donnie Griggs, *Small Town Jesus: Taking the gospel mission seriously in seemingly unimportant places* (Damascus, MD: EverTruth, 2016), p. 18

11 Barna Group, *More Than Multisite: Inside Today's Methods and Models for Launching New Congregations* (Ventura, CA: The Barna Group, 2016), p. 9.

12 Geoff Surratt, Greg Ligon, and Warren Bird, *A Multi-Site Church Road Trip* (Grand Rapids: Zondervan), 2009), p. 15.

13 Warren Bird, *Leadership Network/Generis Multisite Church Scorecard: Faster Growth, More New Believers and Greater Lay Participation* (Leadership Network, 2014), p. 9, accessed January 10, 2019, https://www.beboldacademy.org/images/uploads/Multisite_Church_Scorecard_Report_v2.pdf.

14 Surratt, Ligon, and Bird, *A Multi-Site Church Road Trip, p. 3.*

15 Dave Travis, "10 Trends of the Multisite Church Movement," Aspen Group, Nov. 14, 2017, https://www.aspengroup.com/blog/10-trends-of-the-multisite-church-movement

16 Glenn Daman, *The Forgotten Church: Why Rural Ministry Matters for Every Church in America* (Chicago, IL: Moody Publishers, 2018), p. 7.

17 The 2010 U.S. Religion Census is a source for religious data at the county level. It reports the number of congregations in every U.S. county equivalent to each of the 236 faith groups. http://www.usreligioncensus.org

18 Tena Stone and Chrissy Schaeffer, "Rural Matters: A Focus on Church Planting in Rural America," paper presented at Rural Matters Conference, Sachse, Texas, September 19-20, 2017. (The Rural Matters Conference is a two-day gathering that focuses on affirming, strengthening and inspiring the rural pastor and church leaders, while facilitating the need to plant vibrant churches in rural communities.) https://www.bgcruralmatters.com/rural-matters-conference-2017/

19   Stone and Schaeffer, p. 13.

20   Scott McConnel, *Multi-Site Churches: Guidance for the Movement's Next Generation* (Nashville: B&H Publishing Group, 2009), pp. 6-8.

21   Brad House and Gregg Allison, *Multichurch: Exploring the Future of Multisite* (Grand Rapids: Harper Collins Publishers, 2017), pp. 47-51.

22   "Career Opportunities," *Bethel Church*, accessed January 10, 2019, http://bethel.ag/career-opportunities/. A campus pastor is the local leader of a Bethel Church location. He/She provides pastoral care, discipleship, and ministry training and execution, along with conducting weekly church services.

23   *More Than Multisite: Inside Today's Methods and Models for Launching New Congregations* (Ventura, CA: The Barna Group, 2016), p. 10.

24   Ibid., pp. 11-15.

25   Surratt, Ligon, and Bird, *Multi-site Church Road Trip*, pp. 14-15.

26   Surratt, Ligon, and Bird, *A Multi-Site Church Road Trip*, pp. 203-204.

27   Ibid., pp. 149-151.

28   Ibid., pp. 204-205.

29   "How We Help Multisite," Leadership Network, 2019. Accessed January 18, 2019. http://leadnet.org/how-we-help/multisite/

30   onathan Leeman, "Twenty-Two Problems with Multi-site Churches," 9Marks, October 1, 2014, https://www.9marks.org/article/twenty-two-problems-with-multi-site-churches/

31   Brad House and Gregg Allison, *Multichurch: Exploring the Future of Multisite* (Grand Rapids: Harper Collins, 2017), p. 32.

32   Surratt, Ligon, and Bird, *A Multi-Site Church Road Trip*, pp. 201.

33   House and Allison, pp. 32-33.

34   Darrel Grant Gaines, "One Church in One Location: Questioning the Biblical, Theological, and Historical Claims of the Multi-site Church Movement," (PhD diss., Southern Baptist Theological Seminary, 2012), p. 98, accessed January 18, 2019.

35   Gaines, 99-101. He cites Vincent Branick, *The House Church in the Writings of Paul*, Zacchaeus Studies: New Testament (Wilmington, DE: Michael Glazier, 1989); Stanley Kent Stowers, "Social Status, Public

Speaking and Private Teaching: The Circumstances of Paul's Preaching Activity," *Novum Testamentum* 26, no. 1(1984): 65; Jerome Murphy-O'Connor, *St. Paul's Corinth: Texts and Archaeology*, 3rd ed. (Collegeville, MN: Liturgical, 2002); and L. Michael White, *Building God's House in the Roman World: Architectural Adaptation among Pagans, Jews, and Christians*, (Baltimore: John Hopkins University Press, 1990).

36   Ibid., pp. 101-102.

37   David D'Angelo and Ryan Stigile, *Multisite Church Pitfalls: 7 Dangers You Cannot Afford to Ignore* (Virginia Beach, VA: Createspace Publishing, 2016) p. 1.

38   "Locations," Bethel Church, accessed December 21, 2018, http://bethel.ag/locations/

39   "Home Page," Bethel Church, accessed January 19, 2019, http://bethel.ag

40   Carol Anne Alexander, "Missional Leadership: A Christian Response to Cultural Shifts, Authority Structures and Moral Ambiguities in Contemporary Western Society," (PhD diss., Bangor University, 2010), accessed December 21, 2018, p. 52.

41   D'Angelo and Stigile, p. 2.

42   "Vision Sunday—1.7.2018," YouTube, accessed January 19, 2019, https://www.youtube.com/watch?v=nVCsPI8YxRs; "Bethel Church—Kadoka," Facebook, accessed January 19, 2019, https://www.facebook.com/search/top/?q=bethel%20church%20-%20kadoka&epa=SEARCH_BOX

43   House and Allison, p. 25.

44   Alexander, pp. 52-53.

45   D'Angelo and Stigile, p. 18.

46   Ibid., p. 27.

47   House and Allison, p. 59.

48   D'Angelo and Stigile, p. 27.

49   D'Angelo and Stigile, p. 29.

50   Ibid., p. 33.

51   House and Allison, p. 130.

52   See Thabiti Anyabwile, "Multi-Site Churches Are from the Devil," *The Gospel Coalition*, September 27, 2011, https://www.thegospelcoalition. org/blogs/thabiti-anyabwile/multi-site-churches-are-from-the-devil/ and Johnathan Leeman, "Twenty-Two Problems with Multi-site Churches," *9 Marks*, October 1, 2014, https://www.9marks.org/article/ twenty-two-problems-with-multi-site-churches/

53   House and Allison, p. 78.

54   Ibid., p. 81.

55   House and Allison, p. 81.

56   Brian Nathaniel Frye, *"The Multi-Site Church Phenomenon in North America: 1950-2010"* (PhD diss., The Southern Baptist Theological Seminary, 2011), p. 237 [quoting Sydney Greidanus, "Preaching from Paul Today" from *Dictionary of Paul and His Letters*, ed. Gerald F. Hawthorne, Ralph P. Martin, and Daniel G. Reid (Downers Grove, IL: InterVarsity, 1993), p. 738].

57   House and Allison, p. 84.

58   Surratt, Ligon, and Bird, *A Multi-Site Church Road Trip*, p. 203.

59   House and Alison, p. 86.

60   Surratt, Ligon, and Bird, pp. 203-204.

61   Os Guinness, *The Call* (Nashville: Thomas Nelson, 2003), p. 5.

ACKNOWLEDGMENTS

I am incredibly grateful for the opportunity to have written this book. Completing it would not have been possible without the support of my wife, Melanie. She is a true champion of ministry and my absolute best friend and partner in life. And to my children, Eli and Hannah, thank you for your love and encouragement as I have endeavored to share our story and experience.

Portions of this book are formed from my master's thesis and my personal observations through the years of ministry. The stories shared within these pages are mostly captured from the season of life where I was the Lead Pastor of Bethel Church in South Dakota. The people of Bethel Church are true pioneers. Their ability to adapt, change, take risks, and expand the Kingdom are immeasurable. Thank you for taking a risk on a young pastor and your willingness to dream big!

Over the years I have sought out mentors and God has brought others across my path. Some are mentioned in this book and others I regularly reflect upon their wisdom in my daily ministry. Mentors are rarely honored, but let me say, thank you to those who took the time to speak into my life, leadership and ministry. I am grateful for the collective impact of their lives upon mine.

RESOURCES

Connect with Gerad for coaching, consulting, and
additional copies of *The Forgotten Field* at
www.geradstrong.com
or
www.forgottenfieldbook.com

COACHING & CONSULTING

Gerad Strong's personal experience, education, and national engagement can bring value to your situation. Gerad has a unique ability to help leaders contextualize principles to their context and is available for coaching and consulting in the areas of church planting, church revitalization, church succession, multisite development, and leadership.

> I truly believe that God sent me an incredible gift the day I met Gerad Strong. We sensed God was calling us as a church to plant in a rural community near us through multisite. Through strategic coaching Gerad put us in a position to succeed. He helped me as the Lead Pastor in working with everything from building needs, to community engagement, to mentoring our campus pastor. I often recall the words of encouragement and prophetic prayer Gerad spoke over my life which led us to multiply as a church.
>
> Sheldon McGorman
> Lead Pastor WCAG
> Watford City, North Dakota

CHURCH MULTIPLICATION NETWORK

The Church Multiplication Network (CMN) provides training, resources, and relationships you need to ensure a healthy church in your community—and that includes yours! CMN was critical in providing us with the principles needed to plant in our rural locations.

For assistance in training and other resources, visit
www.churchmultiplication.net

ACTS 2 JOURNEY

Alton Garrison's book *A Spirit-Empowered Church* outlines a template for church health that follows the pattern of the early church in the Book of Acts. An accompanying implementation process called the Acts 2 Journey provides clear principles and applications to help you and your team lead a more missional, outward-focused church.

For additional information, visit
acts2journey.com